'Courageous and honest in bringing to the surface the things that people don't want to talk about, but that are in everyone's heart, soul and mind. This book is a fantastic journey through life, combining practical business insights with personal anecdotes: it gives you the opportunity to put yourself in Mike's shoes and reflect on your own life, work, family and society.'

Carlos Hornstein, Associate Dean, London Business School

'An inspirational read. Michael proves no challenge is ever too big. If you want something, you can achieve it – if you're prepared to listen, learn and work hard.'

Alec Stewart OBE, Director of Cricket, Surrey CCC

'*Live, Love, Work, Prosper* is a groundbreaking book which offers a reality check for us all. Mike brings his fascinating experiences to life with inspiration, provocation and loads of fresh ideas. Ultimately, we all want to live as good a life as possible, but often we have our heads down, the years roll by and we lose our way. This book shows how to refocus, refresh and rediscover a clear vision of what we really want and how to make our lives as good as they can be. A revelation.'

Gordon McAlpine, entrepreneur, mentor and author of *Scale Up Millionaire*

'A clever, complex analysis of the theory of incremental achievement, and an elegant exposition of why love makes life worth living.'

Alastair Stewart OBE

Michael Tobin is one of Britain's most successful and inspirational business leaders.'

Gavin Esler

nspirational, humbling and emotional. Great guidance from
unconventional and sensitive man who has gone through
ceptional experiences. Stories and innovative thoughts that
n help all of us make our journey through life a happier
ie.'

Michel Taride, Group President,
Hertz Rent-a-Car International

When it comes to using technology, do you control it, or
oes it control you? This book addresses the challenge
very executive faces most days – how to balance family
d business with the ever-increasing demands of a 24/7
chnology-driven society. You may not agree with everything
at Michael Tobin recommends. In fact, you may even
sagree with much of it, but this book will certainly make
u stop and think about how you currently deal with
ese challenges and how you can control and benefit from
chnological innovation in all aspects of your life.'

Stephen Murphy, DJO Global

# LIVE
# LOVE
# WORK
# PROSPER

## A FRESH APPROACH
## TO INTEGRATING
## LIFE AND WORK

MICHAEL TOBIN OBE

Third Millennium
Publishing

First published in Great Britain in 2018 by
Third Millennium Publishing, an imprint of
PROFILE BOOKS LTD
3 Holford Yard
Bevin Way
London WC1X 9HD
*www.profilebooks.com*

1 3 5 7 9 10 8 6 4 2

A CIP catalogue record for this book is
available from the British Library.

ISBN (pb): 978 1 78125 876 7
ISBN (hb): 978 1 78125 888 0

Text design by Sue Lamble
*sue@lambledesign.demon.co.uk*
Typeset in Sabon by MacGuru Ltd

Printed and bound in Great Britain by Clays, St Ives plc

FSC
www.fsc.org
MIX
Paper from
responsible sources
FSC® C018072

To my wife Shalina, whose love and support is
the rock of everything I do, and allows me to
integrate my work and life seamlessly.

# Contents

# CONTENTS

# Introduction

*'There is no learning without some difficulty and fumbling. If you want to keep on learning, you must keep on risking failure all your life.'*

John W. Gardner

In the summer of 2016, one of the UK's hottest ever, I ran a marathon. Every day. For 40 days. Afterwards, and definitely during every single one of those 40 back-to-back marathons, I wondered why on earth I had allowed myself to come up with such an insane idea.

I knew exactly when it was, even if I didn't know why. I had been to a dinner at the House of Lords for the Prince's Trust, a charity I'd been involved with for many years, and which was about to celebrate its 40th anniversary. Somewhere between the main course and coffee, one of the speakers had challenged us to come up with an original way of raising the Trust's profile, and funds, during the jubilee year.

I had been placed on the top table next to the speakers' podium. I casually mentioned to the person sitting next to me that I had been thinking about running another London marathon, and maybe I could do it for the Trust. 'You should do 40 marathons, then, since it's the 40th anniversary,' he said jokingly. 'OK,' I replied, 'that's crazy, but maybe...' Then he added, 'And you should do it in 40 days.' Without much reflection I agreed. What I hadn't realised was that this had been overhead by someone else on the table, who was the next speaker on the podium and duly announced to the entire room and the world beyond that Michael Tobin had just agreed to run 26.2188 miles every day for the best part of six weeks.

The audience, of course, cheered. My wife Shalina, on the other hand, thought this was quite possibly the most stupid, irresponsible idea she had ever heard. But there was no way I could escape. I had unwittingly thrown down my own gauntlet, and if I were to back out of the challenge I would not only be letting the Prince's Trust down, but also, to be honest, be subjecting myself to an excruciatingly humiliating experience, possibly one tiny notch down from jilting the bride at the altar. I was pre-committed.

So it was that in the wee small hours of July and August I was pounding the pavements of London – to fulfil my goal and still complete everything else I needed for my business activities. And since I had a full-on work schedule, and no support team to back me up (and knew Shalina would really not appreciate me being away for a month and a half for this crazy notion), I ran the whole thing around London, starting and finishing at my home in Bermondsey each of those 40 days.

I would get up at 2.30 am, start running at 3.30 am and finish around five hours later. After that I collapsed into an ice bath, ate a lunch-sized breakfast and began work. Most mornings I followed a circular route from home, zigzagging across most of the Thames bridges, looping round through the London parks – Battersea, Hyde and Regent's – and across to Shoreditch, the City, Tower Bridge and finally back home.

On other days I would run in a way that allowed me to end

up at the offices of some of my key sponsors, so I could tell their staff at the start of their day why I was running and thank them for their support.

One morning I chaired the AGM of a listed company in my running gear. Initially a number of the shareholders were shocked. But once they heard my story they warmed to me (and therefore the company) and some of them bought even more shares.

While I was running I was generally alone out there in the dark. Even during the longer summer days, dawn was still some way off when I set out and 99 per cent of London's 8.6 million residents were tucked up in bed. Apart from a couple of homeless guys, the only other person I saw was Olly Murs shooting a video at four in the morning.

But I never felt lonely. I might have been physically on my own, but thanks to technology I was among friends. There were no incoming phone calls to distract me, so I streamed each marathon, and via the Periscope app could see when people following me were up and awake around the world. Many would 'like' my livestream and those tiny little heart signs were hugely motivating. It was immensely reassuring to know that other human beings were cheering me on, even if they were on different continents. It brought the experience alive.

People often said to me that I must have benefited from having all those hours to think. They told me that running always cleared their mind. The truth is that most of the time the only thing I was capable of thinking about was just how much my body, my legs and especially my feet hurt. It was super painful. The blisters and the blood were particularly unpleasant – my first pair of trainers had to be binned on Day 5.

To overcome the pain I concentrated on making it to the next lamppost, the next corner, the next bridge. There wasn't much time for calm cogitation and deliberation. And if I did get a thought into my mind, I was running for so many hours that I usually overthought the problem to exhaustion.

It was only afterwards, having run that last, blissful, 40th marathon, that I could try to analyse what the whole thing had meant to me.

A few months later I had the chance to share my experience with Richard Whitehead. Richard is an extraordinary athlete, a double-amputee, a multi-medalled Paralympian, and, to date, the world record holder at both 200 metres and the marathon in his category. He had just picked up a gold and silver in Rio to add to the gold he had won in London four years earlier. In 2013, he had also run 40 marathons in 40 days, not going round in circles like me, but in a straight(ish) line from John O'Groats to Land's End.

His personal inspiration had come from watching a documentary about the runner Terry Fox, an amputee and cancer sufferer who tried to run the whole way across Canada in 1980. Terry Fox failed in his endeavour – his illness forced him to abandon his attempt after 143 days, and he died shortly afterwards – but he created huge awareness of cancer. In Richard's phrase, Terry Fox had 'turned on his light', and he stored that memory and drew on it when he was looking for a way to inspire others. He told me it was all about a door opening and having the confidence and being brave enough to take the first step through that door.

Richard and I talked about how technology could liberate you. For Richard it was the state-of-the-art technology of his running prosthetics and carbon-fibre feet that allowed him to achieve his goals; for me it was the Periscope app that had nursed me through the marathons.

And we talked about family. Richard took on his challenge only months after the arrival of his first baby, Zarah. He said that the family had proved to be a strong, supportive team, and that his mum and dad had instilled in him the core values of earning the right to succeed. Following the marathons, he understood more than ever how important those relationships were. It had changed his perceptions about life and family.

I understood all about that.

Over the previous couple of years I had been through my own significant shift in perceptions. In October 2014, I had parted company with TelecityGroup, the company I had led, and frankly resurrected, taking it from near bankruptcy up towards the top end of the FTSE 250.

After nearly a decade and a half of single-minded, all-consuming commitment, graft, dedication and imagination working for one company, I was out on my own. It was life-changing, for sure. But also life-affirming and liberating in the same way that I have always found technology to be liberating, not constricting.

But unfortunately there had been casualties along the way, not least my family. Working 24/7, concentrating on work and business success to the exclusion of relationships at home, wreaked havoc. My marriage failed, with all the damage that caused to my ex-wife, our three children, and me. Now, remarried, I wanted to understand how it might be possible to achieve both work success and a happy emotional life.

Another trigger for this book was the death in 2013 of Nelson Mandela. He represented for me – as he did for so many others – someone who embodied the vital qualities of a great leader: integrity, strength, forgiveness. He was committed, dignified, humble, human, humorous. I had named my son Nelson after him.

I had a conversation with a South African friend – a man who had lived much of his life in South Africa, and who had known Mandela better than almost anyone. He mentioned in passing that Mandela's greatest regret was not about spending so long in captivity but about the state of his own family – that he had two failed marriages and that his children were squabbling over his legacy even before his death. This really struck home with me. Home being the operative word.

I had been dealing with all the inevitable, difficult fallout of my divorce. But now I was in a new marriage with all the promise of a fresh start. And my work was going well. I had received an OBE from the Queen. There was a discrepancy between success in one field and a significant failure in the other. There had to be lessons to learn that could feed into both my business and personal lives.

Everything that happened made me reassess who I was and how I had been operating for virtually all my adult life. Although I trusted my core beliefs and principles, I had the chance to review my entire philosophy, especially the integration of work, life and love.

As I talked with friends and colleagues about this idea of business and family, and family and business, there was immediate recognition. As soon as I started mentioning these thoughts, their eyes would light up. 'My God, I can relate to that.' They had never thought about work and life and love as a continuum. It had all been neatly parcelled up, separated out, kept in discrete containers (or silos, in that particularly annoying business-speak term). Everything I said was very *familiar* to them. It was about family and work.

These conversations reinforced my belief that there is no such thing as the much-vaunted work/life divide. Rather than thinking in terms of a divide – something that reduces and diminishes both work and life – it should in fact be a powerful *multiplier*. In other words, work, life – and love – can draw on the strengths of each other to create, and enhance, an integrated, potent way of existing, a proper prosperity in the true meaning of the word: not just material wealth, but a flourishing well-being.

In this book I will explain how I re-evaluated (and 'value' is the key part of that word) each of those elements – life, love, work and prosperity – with a new, and I hope more mature, more relevant, perspective.

One of my mantras has always been 'Love it, leave it or change it.'

This book will, I hope, *enlighten* your way of doing business at the same time as *enlivening* your whole way of living.

# Part I

## LIVE

# Chapter 1

# LIVE AND KICKING

## The reality of never switching off

*'Rather than the choice to consciously disconnect,*
*there's much more of a trend of choosing who*
*to connect with and in what context.'*

Emily White, COO, Snapchat

A couple of years ago I was invited to Barcelona to deliver a keynote speech on how technology has influenced education. As I was speaking I explained that the average 14-year-old in Western Europe is able to absorb up to four hours of content for every hour they are actively absorbing content. They can come home, put the TV on, open up their laptop, text a friend, send out a message on Snapchat and listen to their favourite music. All at the same time.

At this point a woman jumped up in the audience and blurted out, 'Are you actually condoning the fact that teenagers today spend all their time on gadgets?' I was a little taken aback, as we had not reached the Q&A session yet, but I answered, '*Señora*, I presume – given the anger in your voice – that you have a 14-year-old at home who "suffers" from this phenomenon?' She replied, 'Yes, my daughter!'

I paused for a moment and then said, 'Imagine that your daughter comes home from school, fires up her iPad to start doing her homework online, switches on the TV to watch a Natural History Channel feature about the Phoenicians, texts her friend in the school Maths club with the solution to a particularly tricky calculus question, and pops her headphones on to listen to Rosetta Stone teaching her Mandarin. You would be inviting all your neighbours round to witness your star child!' She sat down slowly, nodding in agreement. 'It's not the technology we should be angry with,' I continued. 'It's the *content* we should be concerned about.'

# DON'T BLAME THE TECHNOLOGY

I never ever switch off my mobile phone. It is my work phone as well as my personal phone and is with me at all times. It sits within easy reach every single moment of my life. I leave it on in front of me in every meeting.

People, amazingly (or at least amazingly to me), are still quite shocked to hear that. They think it is rather rude. 'What about when you are on holiday?' they ask. 'Well, even on my honeymoon my phone was there.' It's true: I never turn it off, although I do have the good manners to mute it during school concerts, weddings, funerals and awards ceremonies.

I am astonished how many people still find this a difficult concept to grasp and continue to think – over twenty years since it became a commonplace accessory – that the mobile phone is an encumbrance, even a curse.

I see it the other way round. For me the phone is hugely liberating. I believe technology frees rather than chains us. If my phone is not to hand, or tucked away in my bag, there is a piece of my brain engaged with a constant nagging doubt: is there a problem out there that I could be dealing with, that I *should* be dealing with? Because I don't know the answer, I am wasting some valuable synaptic energy on thinking about that rather than concentrating on the meeting or the issue in front of me. But if I can see my phone and it is not flashing, my brain is completely free.

So as long as my mind is not focusing on what **might** be happening, it can focus on what is happening – and that, to my mind, literally, is far more effective: a reverse logic perhaps, but also a total integration of the real and virtual world, 24/7. Mobile technology, as the name suggests, allows you to communicate while you are in motion.

## ON THE MOVE

When I left TelecityGroup in 2014, it was the first time I had been outside that company for nearly a decade and a half. It was a strange experience. I no longer had a physical office, even though I had frequently been away from my office on business trips, and when I was there my door was always open, so it was never a closed space.

I now did not have the support of a dedicated media and marketing team who, in the run-up to a presentation, a pitch or a talk, could knock me up a set of PowerPoint slides in advance. That was proper delegation; although I *could* have created those slides, there were guys on the team who were far more competent with and more imaginative about using PowerPoint, and would always do a far better job than me. Since October 2014 I've been doing them myself. I learnt fast.

Apart from that, leaving the company wasn't too much of a drastic change, because I had always done so much of my own support work. I know some senior executives who have suddenly found themselves outside the comfort zone of an office (through redundancy, boardroom bust-ups, retirement or simply taking their eye off the ball) and been completely bamboozled and disorientated without the support of a calm, efficient PA, an accounts department and the rest of their back-of-house team.

I had always – thanks to my friendly smartphone – done all my own diarising and travel arrangements. I had never had a PA. So being out on my own was pretty much the same routine. I was risking more, because I had no guaranteed income stream, but as I had always run my own office I felt confident in my own abilities to survive out there in the real world.

Within two years I was on the board or was the chairman of a dozen or more companies, and still able to boost my involvement with my favourite charities. I could pick and choose how and where to work, when to sleep, and when to stay awake. When I wanted to go on a trip to India to visit my wife Shalina's family, there was no one telling me I couldn't take the time off – it happened to be a lull in the round of board meetings – and I simply worked and made the calls I needed to place from there.

In the same way, I decided to tackle my 40 back-to-back marathons in July and August 2016 because that was a point in the year when there were the fewest number of board meetings (because naturally you wouldn't want them to clash with popping over to the villa in Tuscany or the beach house in the Hamptons). July and August were quiet on that front, but hot in climate terms, hence my early morning starts. And when necessary I could run (no pun intended) meetings mid-marathon. I 'attended' one board meeting in Hong Kong by phone while I was running round London, and my board member colleagues didn't believe me until I dialled back in on Skype and they saw me run across Tower Bridge.

## WHAT IS NEVER SWITCHING OFF?

'Switched on', as a phrase, generally has a positive connotation, being alert and responsive to what's going on around you. 'Switched off', conversely, has the sense of a disconnect, of not paying attention, being virtually comatose. 'Switching off from work' was shorthand for leaving the drudgery and hassle of the working day behind, and going out and enjoying yourself.

How do you 'switch off'? For some people it's having a meal with friends and family. Or maybe baking, playing a round of golf or going down the pub. For others it's grabbing a tub of Ben & Jerry's and slumping back on the sofa with a boxset of *The Missing* or *Orange is the New Black*.

But that word 'switch' is like a light, with just two settings, on and off. We no longer live in such a binary world.

Most of the kids I know, as I told the conference in Barcelona, are able to switch **off** by switching **on** their iPad, playing a game, Snapchatting or watching YouTube clips.

That's because technology is omnipresent. So you can watch that movie, play a game and check your mails and texts at the same time, **in** the same time. Someone watching you tap your tablet screen has no idea what function, what task, you are engaged in.

Everyone, but everyone, complains about the amount of time kids spend on technology, as if it's a bad thing. Technology is not the problem, people are. We teach our children in a linear fashion. You have Maths from 9.15 to 10.15, English from 10.15 to 11.15, Design and Technology up to lunchtime. The reality is that kids are used to having four hours' content within every actual hour of their lives. They have learnt the skill of going in and out of focus. Not parallel multi-tasking but *serial* multi-tasking.

## THE DEMISE OF 9 TO 5

The concept of the 9-to-5 job seems to have been with us since time immemorial, although it is, of course, a by-product of the modern industrial age. In pre-industrial times you got up with the dawn and cracked on. Natural light was important: you worked from first light to dusk. Otherwise, you and your family would starve.

But 9 to 5 is now ready to be consigned to the history books. It is becoming – in reality has already become – a thing of the past. We need to remain connected to business and leisure all the time. There is no going back.

The irreparable cracks in that anachronistic structure appeared partly as a result of changes in employment norms – the rise of freelance and self-employed, outsourced and home-based workers – but also out of a realisation that genuinely useful and creative thinking was not always best served by being stuck inside a schedule, or a cubicle. Douglas Coupland, that ever-astute observer of social trends (and the author who popularised the terms 'Generation X' and 'McJob'), has said:

*The 9 to 5 is barbaric. I really believe that. I think one day we will look back at 9-to-5 employment in a similar way to how we see child labour in the nineteenth century. The future will not have the 9 till 5. Instead, the whole day will be interspersed with other parts of your life.*

In the past five years, the number of people working remotely, telecommuting, has soared. The previous geographical, physical constraints of working have been eradicated. I am chairman of a company whose sole objective is to provide high-speed broadband via satellite to residents of remote areas who will never see a strand of fibre come into the home. Being connected is becoming a right in the whole world, not just the developed world, right up there alongside running water.

But that does have an impact on our relationships with our family. Recent research (by Pullman Hotels/Ipsos) has revealed that 86 per cent of people take their work mobile on holiday, and 40 per cent pack their work laptop. Nearly three quarters of them extend their work into their holiday time.

Nearly half (48 per cent) of the respondents admitted that they checked their business emails before leaving for work in the morning (to be honest I was surprised it was only 48 per cent...) and 40 per cent would check their mail in bed before they went to sleep.

Among the findings behind this blurring of distinctions between work and home, various reasons were given – with some respondents citing all of them!

O  62 per cent said their work required a high level of involvement.

O  28 per cent wanted to be seen by their bosses to be showing extra commitment.

O  14 per cent justified it by saying everyone else at work did the same.

I bet none of them felt particularly happy about giving those answers, since they were feeling *obliged* to work at home: they were only doing it because they felt it was an essential part of 'being successful', that it was part of the journey towards success.

As a result just over half felt guilty for not spending as much time with their loved ones as they would like. A quarter had been rebuked by their partners for not switching off their phones. And 13 per cent found themselves actually *hiding* the number of out-of-office hours they were putting in, or lying about it, like hiding a drink or drugs problem.

That cannot be a healthy situation: when people start feeling guilty, becoming deceitful and maybe feeling a sense of anger towards their work or, worse, towards their partners, they are not going to be working or living well or positively.

## TECHNOLOGY AS LIBERATION NOT INCARCERATION

I have found myself increasingly drawn to working with companies who can use technology to liberate human beings.

I first met Xenios Thrasyvoulou, the CEO of a company called People Per Hour, on a skiing trip with friends. It was a time when Shalina and I were designing the interior of our new house, and wanted to have a 3D walk-through of the house first so we could more easily visualise the space beyond the architect's traditional 2D plans. The cheapest quote we'd had for a video-style presentation was £40,000 – yes, the cheapest quote.

I was telling Xenios about this and he suggested trying his website. He said:

*It's like a reverse eBay for jobs. You put into the website whatever you happen to want, and from anywhere in the world people can quote on the job. You can look at their*

*experience and their portfolio, think about their quotes, drill
down a bit more once you've whittled it down to two or
three. You might not necessarily settle on the cheapest quote,
but you might simply like their style.*

We followed his advice and found a guy somewhere in
Asia – I never knew exactly where, such is the reality of the
cyberworld – who was working nights to put himself through
university, and who created five or six versions of what we
wanted for a tenth of the price. He was happy, and so, believe
me, were we.

I decided to get more involved with People Per Hour: we
looked at the competition, other companies like Ffiver, where
you paid a straightforward £5 for simple tasks like finding
someone to do a Hawaiian dance for a stag party with the
groom's name lipsticked on their chest, silly little ideas like
that. Each of these other companies had their own twist.

We suggested that People Per Hour should be a portal for
all these other companies, a front end like Google, a landing
page that would redirect users to the most appropriate product.
The investors said, 'You're just pushing business and turnover
to our competitors.' Yes, but they would go to those other
sites anyway. This way we could own the front end, monitor
and quantify traffic, and analyse why the best ones were doing
well, all driven by the need to solve a problem through technology. The business continues to thrive, and I am a happy
shareholder.

A different take on the beneficial interface between technology and life is Ultrahaptics, set up by Steve Cliffe, a brilliant
entrepreneur, and Tom Carter, a Bristol University graduate.
Tom was working on creating the sensation of touch through
ultrasound, based on the ultrasonic transducers in car bumpers

which send signals out and back (like a bat) to warn you when you're about to bash into a car parked behind you.

He created an algorithm, with a camera following your hand, that could send out an array of signals at different times to arrive at the same moment on a pinpoint. So you could feel the concentrated signals even though there was nothing physical there. Now you can press a button in mid-air and feel it, even though it doesn't exist. Suddenly there was a sensation of touch, which at that point virtual reality had not yet delivered. A VR headset offered great visuals but no tactile feedback. Now the virtual reality loop could be closed back to a physical sensation. That's the haptics part: 'haptic', a word I certainly wasn't familiar with before, means 'relating to the sense of touch'.

Imagine picking up a mug if you can't physically feel the other side of the mug. It's OK with a glass because you can see your fingers through the glass, and your brain can apply the necessary pressure from muscle memory. But with a mug you can't see or feel the other side. Without any idea of pressure requirement, things will slip down or, conversely, get crushed.

Once you start thinking about the possible applications, they come thick and fast. I was at a hospital for an appointment and had just got into one of the lifts. A doctor walked in after me and said, 'Can you press Floor 3?' I thought, 'Hey, why don't you do it yourself, you lazy so-and-so?' He must have seen the look on my face, because he explained that the single biggest hazard in hospitals is the spread of MRSA from elevator buttons. As he put it, 'Would you like me to be operating on you or maybe your wife next?' So then I wondered, what if the lift button was an ultrasound mid-air button?

A large theme park in the UK was testing this idea for

virtual reality spiders in one part of the tour. Through the VR headset you saw the spiders and then via ultrasound felt them running up your arms and legs. In the test people ripped their headsets off and hurled them down. It was that real. This is really exciting for me, as it brings the physical world and the virtual world together, a bit like work and home life.

## MAKE TECHNOLOGY YOUR FRIEND

I believe that if we actively embrace technology – because it is not going to go away – and take control of it with a positive mindset, then we will actually have a better, more rewarding time with our families. The secret is in managing the information flow and having an inclusive approach. There is an overload of information spewing out towards us every day. By applying a level of triage, just like they do in A&E units, you can put an early, effective filter in place, specifying what is really urgent and what is simple information.

In the same way, creating shorter, more efficient meetings during work time, and setting clear boundaries on what each phase of your time is for, allows you to concentrate on what is important. Technology can do that for you: it already does. If you get your junk settings right, you can let your system divert an enormous amount of irrelevant digital bilge.

More important, of course, is your personal junk filter. You need the courage and confidence to cut through the crap. You are not so important that the world revolves around you. If you are, then you have completely screwed up your recruitment plan for your direct reports. You have employed people who cannot do what you do. You have kept yourself 'essential'. This is not good!

Snapchat's Emily White and Coca-Cola's Wendy Clark have an interesting approach to time management in a hyper-connected world. During a panel at Fortune's Most Powerful Women Summit, White, the COO of Snapchat and a veteran of Instagram, Facebook and Google, said she now relies on her phone more than her computer to get work done. 'You're not just getting information and solving problems; you're getting to communicate in motion like never before,' she commented. 'This is the reason I can have kids and still have a relationship with them, and work in the evenings when I get home [after the kids are in bed].'

For Wendy Clark, the president of 'sparkling brands and strategic marketing' for Coca-Cola North America, being present at work or with her family is the key to living in an over-connected world. 'The thing people want most from you is your focus and attention. You destroy that when you think that you're multi-tasking, because you're not accomplishing either.'

If we use technology to give us more freedom, to liberate our minds (just as I do with my phone), it can actually make us happier rather than angrier. Work should be your friend, not the enemy. Technology can be your best friend.

## AUGMENTING REALITY

To take this idea further, how far can we allow technology to be part of our lives? Is there a limit, a point where it really does become counter-productive? I don't know yet, because we have barely started to scrape the surface of the benefits of technology and how it can help shape a more effective, less random, happier life.

That's what I discovered when working with Ultrahaptics. For example, if you are driving, imagine the sound system volume control button hovering just by your steering wheel. It doesn't exist as a 3D object, it's a heads-up virtual button, but when you put your finger on it you get a physical response, maybe even a sound, and can adjust the volume while never taking your eyes off the road. The key is in getting the physical feedback, because we constantly need to know how other people feel about us; we are steered by praise or disapproval.

That feedback from technology is the way forward. Rather than technology isolating us, it can make us feel in touch with other human beings – just as the Periscope app stopped me feeling lonely by feeding me messages of support from around the world when I was running my 40 marathons in the middle of the night.

Of course, Periscope or FaceTime or Skype can never replace the extraordinary reality and dynamism of a face-to-face conversation. But maybe it can step in when that kind of a conversation is impossible. There are many people who would love any kind of human contact – the sound of their voice, or just a smiley emoticon on a text – because they lack that in their own lives. We know the great work that the Samaritans do. Similarly, the Silver Line is a phone line staffed by volunteers who talk to elderly people who find themselves with few friends and hampered by mobility problems.

Yet sometimes being in the same room and *having* to make stilted conversation can be excruciating – during a marriage breakdown, maybe. At that point, dealing by text would be far less destructive.

I know first-hand, sadly, the lack of 'contribution' I made to enrich my own kids' lives when I was physically present but my head was elsewhere. Pure physical presence is not on its own enough if your mind is not there. If you are in the zone but online, could that be a better solution than being there but zoned out – another example of technology potentially liberating rather than incarcerating.

Our communal minds have not yet caught up with this concept. Take driving and texting. That is clearly a dangerous, if not downright stupid, thing to do, since if you are texting and looking down at your mobile's screen rather than concentrating on the road, the potential results are self-evident. And quite rightly the laws have been changed in this regard.

Now that driverless cars are imminent, there will have to be a shift in perception. If it is OK to sit in the 'driver's' seat while the car takes control and takes care of all the calculations and judgements to do with speed, acceleration, distance that we do as drivers, then we should be able to have a drink, send a text, read a book. But at this point, that is not acceptable either by law or in the public perception. So we can delegate functions to technology, but not enjoy the benefits. We have to sit there *as if* we were driving, although we are not. This will change, but there is a way to go yet.

## ALLOWING AI TO TAKE THE STRAIN

There's a scene in *The Imitation Game*, the film about Alan Turing and the Enigma code, in which Alan Turing is being interviewed by the police. During the course of the interview the policeman asks him, 'Can computers think?' 'It depends,' Turing answers, 'what "think" is.' If thinking is a series of reasonings and 'what if's, then maybe it can. The key is whether the computer can learn from previous results, so it can predict and predetermine the best way forwards. At what point do the binary 1s and 0s grow to a level at which the digital becomes virtually analogue?

Frankly, looking at the way we human beings constantly fail to learn from experience and blunder on making the same mistakes as we, and generations before us, have always done, then maybe a computer's more rational thinking might be more beneficial. And then perhaps artificial intelligence gets to be so good that it becomes – like HAL, the computer in *2001: A Space Odyssey* – defensive of its own abilities. We are not at that point yet, but we are significantly along the way towards it. I believe computers will 'defend' themselves against our wishes within twenty years.

Perhaps we need to explore the idea of man and machines, where technology and humans merge. At one level, Richard Whitehead, as a supreme Paralympian, has already done that, with his prosthetics and carbon-fibre feet.

I have often advocated microchipping for humans, in exactly the same way we microchip pets. If I was involved in a car accident, I would far rather the paramedics could quickly scan my chip and instantly know my blood type, whether I was allergic to penicillin and any relevant medical history so that they could apply instant treatment rather than scrabbling through my blood-stained wallet trying to decipher an ID card in pitch darkness on a motorway hard shoulder – if, indeed, I was even carrying an ID card. If we could become our own devices, and scan our own hand, then we would have no need for the devices we either lose and have to relocate on Find My iPhone, or leave behind in airport lounges after one selfie too many (confession time: I did just that in New York, after grabbing a selfie with Michael Bublé).

What we need to do is understand that technology in its immediacy can bring positivity rather than negativity.

Leadership coach Chantal Burns, who created the State of Mind Index (SOMi), has observed that 'Happiness is a state of mind and the great news is that the only thing that stops us from feeling happy, content and confident right now is the mistaken belief that something other than your own thinking can determine how you feel. Happiness is quite literally available in an instant.'

Using technology wisely and well can help us to take control of our own happiness by giving us mastery over when and how we work. This can be a powerful force for good.

## QR: AUGMENTED DISCOVERY

Click on the QR code at the end of this chapter. You'll instantly download clips of me telling you more about each of these key points:

- Understand that technology frees us rather than ties us up. It is hugely liberating. By being in touch 24/7, there is no pent-up fear of problems you are not aware off sitting out there waiting to take you by surprise or screw up your best-laid plans – plans based on the information you *thought* you had access to.

- Focus on what is actually happening, not what might be happening. This is the most effective use of time, energy and money. Never switching off means you are permanently switched *on*.

- Remember: technology (and hence work) is a friend, not an enemy. Never feel guilty about working, and never hide it from your family. Let them know what you are working on, even if they don't need all the detail.

- Make sure you are in charge of when and how you work. You need to manage information flow. It's easy to fall behind the cutting edge of technology. Stay ahead of it.

*'Eventually everything connects – people, ideas, objects. The quality of the connections is the key to quality per se.'*

Charles Eames

# Chapter 2

# LIVE HAPPILY

## Every minute counts

*'Count your age by friends, not years.*
*Count your life by smiles, not tears.'*

John Lennon

A few years ago I acquired a business in Ireland from an Argentinian called Eduardo, a real gentleman. We were trying to cut the deal, which for him – according to what he told me some time later – was probably the best deal of his life. He had bought a data centre company when it was on the verge of going bankrupt, picking it up for pretty much nothing. He had put in something like a million euros of investment, and two or three years later my company, TelecityGroup, bought it off him for at least 90 times that investment. Not surprisingly he looked back on that deal with some pleasure: and it also happened to be a really good deal for TelecityGroup. We made six times our money on it.

While we were in mid-negotiation, I was trying very hard not to let him sell the company on the open market, in order to keep control of the process. We were aiming to close the deal on a Friday. I knew that as a practising Jew he would not do a deal during the Sabbath, and I also knew that on that particular Friday he was up in Scotland playing golf, and it was mid-winter. So I phoned him around midday and said, 'I'm aware it is going to be an earlier sunset where you are compared to where I am, so what's my drop-dead date to get you the final proposal?' He said, 'Michael, get it to me by 2.30 absolute latest.' So I moved heaven and earth to complete all the paperwork, made the deadline and got the deal.

We subsequently became good friends. Shalina and I went to his daughter's wedding in Buenos Aires, where we talked about this particular deal. He said the reason he trusted me, and why he had to say no to any other offers, was his belief that I was going to follow through on the proposal, in which I had promised to retain the management team, whom he wanted me to look after. Then he told me that the one thing which really convinced him to trust me was that phone call. Simply because I had taken the trouble to think about what time sunset would be that far north. I had dealt with him with an eye for latitudes, not platitudes.

When I was running my 40 marathons in 40 days, I gave a keynote speech – before embarking on the challenge – at an event organised by Eduardo's new company, and he donated the ticket sales and proceeds to the Prince's Trust. The circle of trust continues.

The deal had been fantastic for him, so he was extremely happy with what had happened. We had paid a lot of money for his data centre company, but had in fact made a very wise investment, just at a much higher level. The bottom line was that there was a win/win but, although he won at a relatively higher level than I had, I wasn't unhappy about that. He had taken a bigger risk earlier in the cycle. It made me realise that happiness in business doesn't have to be an equal thing. It is genuinely relative to your expectations and your context. And so it is in life.

# SUCCESS DOES NOT MAKE US HAPPY

As a society, we are extremely focused on creating success, and we often define our happiness in terms of how much success we create. We have become obsessed by the perception that happiness is driven by success:

O  If I can get promotion I will be happy.

O  If I am successful I will be happy.

O  If I can increase the share price of my company by a factor of 12 I will be considered a success, and therefore I will be happy.

These are all false premises. Happiness is not driven by success. Our relativisation of success is constant in everything we do: the more successful we become, the more the bar for our definition of success rises, making it harder to succeed. That's great for business, but if your happiness hinges on that, you will ultimately be unhappy. It's the law of big numbers. The higher the bar, the tougher the challenge, but the happiness level doesn't increase in proportion.

When I was CEO of TelecityGroup, there was one day when the stock market took a dive and the company's share price fell sharply (everybody's share price plummeted that particular day), so I was initially very unhappy. The market had crashed. My spirits followed suit.

But at the very point I was at my most depressed, a raft of investors and analysts were calling me and saying, 'Mike, chill out. I am not going to be selling today, whatever the share price is at the close of business.'

I realised that if we could finish the day within, say, 3 per cent of where we had started it would in fact have been a relatively good day, 'relatively' being the key word. Nothing would have changed except time moving on, and my own perception of what success was.

Our interpretation of success alters all the time. We are never 'happy', because at the very moment we achieve our expectation, our expectations shift once more, and the definition of what makes us happy moves out of reach yet again.

It is important to define what makes you, personally, happy, because feeling happy is as much physiological as emotional. When you are happy, endorphins are released into your body, which in turn make you far more receptive to outside inputs, more alert and more active, and so, by virtue of these endorphins whizzing around your body and your brain, you have a greater chance of achieving more success.

The equation is simple: the happier you are to begin with, the more successful you will become – the complete opposite of the way we are typically taught to view the world.

## 'THAT'S NOT FAIR': WHY ENVY BREEDS UNHAPPINESS

I recently came across a YouTube clip about an experiment that had been carried out by Frans de Waal, professor of primate behaviour at Emory University in Atlanta, Georgia.

He placed two monkeys in adjacent cages. Each monkey

could clearly see the other one. Now, monkeys love cucumbers but they *really* love grapes. Professor de Waal had asked this pair of monkeys to perform a simple task each, in return for which they got a reward.

One of his assistants gave one of the monkeys a stone and the monkey had to hand the stone back to her. When he did she gave him a reward, a piece of cucumber, and, since monkeys are very fond of a bit of cucumber, he was extremely happy. The monkey then watched her go to the other cage right next door to his.

She gave the second monkey the stone, and got it back. But this time she rewarded the other monkey with... a grape. The first monkey clocked this: 'I did the task and got a piece of cucumber. My mate next door did exactly the same task as I did, and he got a grape, and although I like cucumber, I *love* grapes.' When the assistant gave him the stone again, and then when he handed it back, she only gave him some more cucumber. He started going crazy – completely 'ape', in fact – really annoyed that he didn't get given a grape. This continued until the first monkey started throwing the stone at the assistant in anger.

It's a great example of how win/win situations are all relative, just like my deal with my Argentinian friend. Our first monkey was totally delighted with his cucumber until he saw his chum was getting a grape. Your cucumber is always somebody's else grape.

Why was the monkey getting so agitated? Was it because he was not getting a grape or because the other one *was* getting a grape? As soon as he knew that a grape was on offer, his piece of cucumber was worthless, and I imagine that even if they'd given the second monkey a piece of cucumber the second time around he would not have been placated because he'd know they were only doing that to make it even.

It's like every staff salary review I have ever undertaken. It was something I used to have a go at my management team about all the time, because I could give one person a pay rise and another person a different pay rise. Both would be delighted, until the first guy spoke to the second and found out he had been given twice as much, and was suddenly unhappy – despite having got a pay rise he was happy with in the first place.

# CHANNELLING ANGER TO POSITIVE ENDS

Anger in itself is not an emotion we necessarily have to eradicate completely: it can be a healthy release of pent-up frustration that, once released in the right way, can free up our mind to move on, rather than having the anger fester away inside us.

Anthony Foley, the Munster and Ireland rugby union player and coach, died unexpectedly early at the age of 42 in October 2016. In the tributes that followed, one piece by the BBC's Tom English talked about how in the mid-1990s Munster was 'an irrelevance' when rugby's European Cup started up. They were inconsistent, and no one had any hope of them achieving anything. But Foley, their captain, drove the team on with honesty and ferocious tenacity. 'When Munster suffered a setback he'd tell his team-mates to stick the memory of the loss into what he called the "bitterness bank". He used bitterness in a big way.'

Eventually they made the Heineken Cup final in 2000 and

2002, but lost both. They reached the semi-finals in 2001, 2003 and 2004 and lost each of those too. Finally, finally, they lifted the Cup in 2006: the Bank of Bitterness had paid out.

Rather than getting angry each time they just lost out, Foley saw a value in that loss, and passed on that feeling to his team. Like an alchemist he taught his team-mates how to turn bile into burning determination. No point in dwelling on the bitterness but well worth harnessing the inevitable disappointment, while never forgetting that feeling. Ten minutes from the end of the next final they could remind themselves of how bad they had felt the last time, and raise their game to try and make sure it didn't happen again. Remember how you felt? Bloody angry. Well, take that into the future, as a multiplier, a magnifying glass.

## CONVERTING ANGER BACK TO CALMNESS, AND HAPPINESS

Every year at TelecityGroup I brought in a yogi, Jagdish Parikh, to work with the management team. One of the things he taught them was how to hypnotise themselves – not in the falling asleep or becoming a dog way, but in terms of capturing control.

Jagdish explained that it is actually quite difficult to define who we are. Are we our body? Yes, to some extent: if we didn't have a body, then we couldn't exist. But are we our mind? Yes, but if we didn't have a heart, our mind could not function. Are we our soul? Yes, but we can't quantify that, it's an intangible concept. We are a combination of all things: body, spirit, soul, brain, experience. This combination defines who we are and is not a single physical thing. He told us all: 'Who you really are is none of those but all of those. You are the owner and the manager of all those elements. So if you can get out of your body, and effectively become a "third person", then you will be able to manage and manipulate your thoughts and emotions far more easily from a third party position.'

His theory was that when you are arguing with someone, rowing over some petty problem, if you can stand outside of yourself and look at the argument, you will start laughing because it is so often so ridiculous. I do this a lot. When I find myself taking a stand about something, I trigger a signal that reminds me to become a third person and look at the situation from the outside. Almost always I find what I am doing to be less than optimal. I am sure you will be familiar with the concept of being able to tell others what is the right thing to do while being unable to follow your own advice. It is easier to see the logic when you are disconnected from the situation.

The key, as Jagdish explained to us, is to become aware of when and how your anger is triggered, because if you are conscious of yourself then you can start manipulating your emotions. If you are driving to a meeting and you are late, it seems that you always hit a red light and it always seems to last longer than usual before turning green. Of course, there isn't any difference from any other day. But every red light you hit winds you up even more because you are getting later and later. We never think, 'I should have set out 15 minutes earlier', instead we just think 'bloody red lights'.

Jagdish taught us that a red light can be a trigger for calm; instead of winding you up it could actually de-stress you. We are conditioned to see red as a bad colour, the colour of anger. If you can learn that red is calm, calm is red, you will still be late for your meeting but you will arrive with a much better mood and attitude, more able to move straight into getting the point quickly, rather than wasting time in flustering.

When you are sitting in a meeting and things are going badly, people tend to demonstrate physical signs of frustration, irritation or embarrassment. Their knee might start twitching, or they start drumming their fingers on the table. These are the 'red lights'. What you have to do is work out what your trigger is. Use the trigger as your early warning system; once you can recognise it, you can use it to counteract your instinctive reaction.

One member of our team used to sit right back in his chair on two of its legs, as far back as he could, and because he was worrying about toppling over, and concentrating on his balance, he stopped thinking about what was annoying him.

In my case I don't have a specific overt physical response. Mine is more of a mental reaction. My mind starts to get a bit scrambled. I grow impatient. I am thinking of other things and not what I should really be focusing on. Usually it is because I am trying hard to be tolerant of what I am hearing, even though I don't find it credible. I find myself just listening out for gaps in the conversation when I can have a chance to speak, rather than listening to the content of what is being said.

At a certain moment my patience will pop, but thanks to Jagdish I am now able to sense that moment looming. At that point I reset. I reboot. And think to myself, 'What am I trying to do here?' I distract myself to diffuse my irritation, pick up a coffee pot, move something on the table, look out of the window, to give myself the two or three seconds I need to reset my mind. It makes for a smoother life.

A friend's 12-year-old daughter has come up with a similar technique: when she is getting angry and about to have a blazing ding-dong with her dad, she says 'Liquorice'. It's a common word, but not one you use every day. It's a code word for both of them to stop arguing, and go off to cool down. Being able to think that way at her age is incredibly powerful.

## SPREAD A LITTLE HAPPINESS

By controlling anger, you will feel happier, and be much more productive: how many man hours are wasted at work, and at home, by pointless arguments, futile email wars, muttered disagreements?

Conversely, if you can generate and transmit a sense of happiness and appreciation, everyone can feel the benefit.

Shortly after leaving TelecityGroup I went into the City law firm Jones Day (although I haven't done any business with them, I'm namechecking them for reasons that will become clear). At the front of their building a member of staff was there to open the door for visitors. At the downstairs desk, instead of just handing me a badge and saying 'fourth floor', the receptionist walked me to the lifts. At the fourth floor reception, another staff member greeted me and walked with me to the room where the meeting was going to be held.

As we were walking along I mentioned how nice their offices were, and asked how long they'd been in the building. She said, 'I don't know, I've only been here two years.' While I was sitting waiting for the guy I was meeting to come to the room, she came back, and knocked on the door. She said, 'Sorry to interrupt, but I have just checked and we have been here for nine years, and the offices were refurbished six years ago. I hope that answers your question.' Wow. Off the cuff she had taken the trouble to go that extra step.

Thinking about other people in this way was clearly a pervasive culture throughout the company. The comfort level I felt there was enormous. If we were all like that to our clients, imagine the impact.

It's always possible to show how much you appreciate the people you work with by taking a little extra time outside the hurly-burly of the working day. It just needs a little extra planning, which in itself shows that you value their contribution. There is thought behind this that goes deeper than a box of chocolates.

At one management get-together in Tenerife, I wound up the day's proceedings by saying to the team, 'I would like all of you, every day until the end of this month, to send a thank you message to one other person in this room, copying everybody else in, and remember I want you to do this every morning before 12 o'clock.' Their response of course was, 'Mike, you are absolutely nuts.' But they stuck to it, and each one sent a message to one of the other team members with a 'thank you' for something they had done. It was massively uplifting. People were saying, 'I didn't even realise you knew I did that, I didn't know you appreciated me.' And others said, 'She did *that* for you? Could you do that for me too?' It radiated happiness.

You have to think of different drivers to get people buzzing. It's a fact that most people aren't only incentivised by money, and don't want to move jobs. Engineers, for example, don't necessarily want to be promoted to become the managers of engineering departments; they want to do what they are good at – hands-on engineering. Understanding those motivations and showing that you appreciate them creates happiness.

At TelecityGroup, each year we would celebrate the 10-year work anniversaries of any team members by inviting them and their partners to a black-tie event in the glass dome at the top of London's Gherkin. This was a physical recognition of the fact that they had given 10 years of their working lives to the company.

I would ask the team members' friends to give me some information about them, not the usual 'he's got two kids and a Citroën Picasso', but something along the lines of 'he likes heavy metal and plays the oboe' or 'he coaches his kids' sports team'. In front of the whole room – and there would be dozens of people celebrating 10 years with the company in any given year – I would talk about each of them, using this extra bit of information I had gleaned, things the others didn't know, so I didn't have to mumble the usual clichés.

That worked incredibly well. The experience of having a celebration at the top of an iconic building and a weekend in London on the company was matched by an appreciation of the time taken to make it super personal. The goodwill they felt was paid back to the company in spades.

'Goodwill' may be quantified on a company balance sheet of a company in a merger or acquisition, but, of course, you can't really quantify its full impact. Everyone at those Telecity events appreciated them when they were happening, but the feeling also had a longer-term effect, creating a buffer zone of happiness against any future difficulties, disagreements and conflict.

So why don't we do this at home? Why should there be a difference between how we treat our work colleagues and how we treat our friends and family? We spend hours thinking about what motivates and retains great staff. How much time do we spend thinking about what motivates and retains family members?

It reminds me of one of the stories my sister told me as a kid. The sun and the wind have a bet, looking down at this man walking to work with a coat and a hat. The wind says to the sun, 'I reckon I can get this guy's coat or his hat off.' The wind starts blowing as hard as he can, and of course the harder it blows, the tighter this man closes his coat and holds on to his hat. Then the sun says, 'OK, I will have a go,' sends down his strongest rays and, of course, the man immediately removes his coat and hat because it is so hot. That is the positivity of the smile. Positivity will almost certainly give you a better solution and can drain the venom from a difficult situation – offering a glimmer of a chance that you can pull it back before it descends into a fractious fallout.

This is something I have often struggled with, because I am not very tolerant of people who are unreliable. If someone says to me, 'I will do this', and then they don't, after several occasions I will get upset, and that doesn't help: in fact, it never helps. Positivity is always the better option. I know it is much more productive to try to understand why team members have failed and support them to improve performance. I have had to learn, am still trying to learn, to drink my own Lucozade!

## LOOKING BACK AT A HAPPY LIFE

If you could fast-forward to your last day of life, would you expect all of your life to have been lived in complete happiness? I doubt that anyone would.

What most of us would like to see is that a large proportion of it had been made up of happiness – however we choose to define that – while we would also accept that some slices of our past life involved failure, sadness and unhappiness. You

44

would naturally expect to see a mixture of failure and success; otherwise you would be deluded.

So we have accepted that our 'happiness' includes an element of failure. 'Success' is defined by a period in time. We define success in different slices of time.

If you want your football team to win the league, the likelihood of success may be low and the likelihood of unhappiness – if winning the league is your simple definition of happiness – high. But if you want your team to win just their next game, then you have a much higher likelihood of happiness, and the prospect of another injection of endorphins.

In a business context, there is a powerful lesson to be learnt here: by clearly determining an achievable level of success at the macro level for the company and at the micro level for each individual within it, we may be able to increase the overall sense of achievement, which in turn leads to greater happiness, which in turn, again, will lead to greater success – and avoid burnout.

Emotion, any kind of emotion, is powerful. For me, I can categorise the most powerful emotions as the four Ds:

1 Disgust ('enough is enough')

2 Decision-making ('there is a fork in the road and I have to decide which one to take')

3 Desire ('the thing within in me that drives me onward')

4 Determination ('never giving up').

Channelling these emotions, and steering them all towards the ultimate goal of happiness, is a challenge, but equally a huge opportunity. In business, and in life, we need to accept that **we** are the owners of our ability to be happy. And the more we can spread happiness to others, the happier than makes us feel too.

# QR: AUGMENTED DISCOVERY

Click on the QR code opposite. You'll instantly download clips of me telling you more about each of these key points:

■ Happiness is often defined by success. Why not turn this idea on its head: success is defined by happiness. Happiness has to come first.

■ The happier you are to begin with, the more successful you will become. Happiness releases endorphins – just like physical exercise – which in turn keep you alert and focused.

■ Success is a movable feast: 'success' is the next target. When you achieve that, a new 'success' is in place. It's a never-ending process. Determine realistic targets to boost your sense of achievement.

■ Don't strive for happiness. Happiness is like an orgasm: if you focus on it too much it goes away. Focus on making other people happy – help happiness go viral.

*'For every minute you are angry you lose*
*sixty seconds of happiness.'*

Ralph Waldo Emerson

# Chapter 3

# LIVE DIFFERENTLY

## Looking at life from another angle

*'Be daring, be different, be impractical, be anything
that will assert integrity of purpose and imaginative
vision against the play-it-safers, the creatures of
the commonplace, the slaves of the ordinary.'*

Cecil Beaton

I worked for the same company for the best part of a decade
and a half. Previously the longest I had worked anywhere was
four years, when I was an apprentice.

I worked so long for TelecityGroup because the company
was constantly morphing, and I was involved in every change. I
took it from being a public company on the FTSE down to AIM,
the Alternative Investment Market, and then fully de-listed the
company. I nursed it through a rocky period of survival, before
merging it with our major competitor within the industry. Once
that was complete, I embarked on an acquisitions programme
across multiple countries, relisting it as a FTSE 250 company once
again, followed by further acquisitions and rapid expansion.

Every year the company looked different, and presented me

with a fresh set of problems and opportunities. There was no way on this planet that I would have stayed with the company if it had remained static. I'm not very good with static. So, for far longer than anyone – including myself – could have predicted, I remained at the helm. But the time came when I, and they, needed to move on in separate directions.

## A LINE IS DRAWN

Early in August 2014 I took a call from the company secretary, who told me that the chairman and the head of compliance wanted a meeting with me. I was in the office but the meeting was going to be offsite. I had been in the game too long not to know what this meant. It was a classic ploy I had used myself when arranging a parting of the ways with one of the senior management, bringing in the head of compliance to negotiate a package and holding the meeting offsite in case the person threw a fit. I knew what was going to happen, so I suggested it could be done in a more structured way at the AGM; however, they didn't want to wait.

In many ways this change happened at a less than optimal time. I had recently got married and was reconstructing a new house from top to bottom. But there's never a perfect time for anything. The day you sit around waiting for the perfect moment is when you realise that the opportunity has gone begging. Or, as John Lennon put it, 'Life is what happens to you while you are busy making other plans.'

I got a certain amount of stick for leaving TelecityGroup. There were plenty of highly complimentary newspaper articles and lots of speculation about what had happened. Having just published a book called *Forget Strategy. Get Results*, one or two financial journalists had a pop at me, along the lines of *Forget Strategy. Get Fired*. But all of them said, 'like him or not, great performance'. The shareholders came out in support. I had taken the company from a market capitalisation of £6 million to over £1.5 billion. But I knew that I would soon be forgotten in the Telecity scheme of things. Life moves on. I didn't spend much time worrying about what people thought. I had to get on with this change in my life.

My own experience has taught me that embracing such change, even when that means confronting the unknown at work or tackling problems at home, can lead to positive transformation. Looking at the world from a different angle can help us to evolve, making things better for ourselves, our businesses and our loved ones.

## EVOLUTION IN RELATIONSHIPS

At one point as the CEO I had had to let one of the senior members of my Telecity team leave. It was not a good feeling, because I had recruited him in the first place, been through the whole process of briefing out the description, drawing up a shortlist, running the interviews. I had recruited him for a very specific job, an IPO (Initial Public Offering), which demanded an equally specific set of skills.

But time had passed, the company's and my objectives had changed and the many excellent skills I had originally needed, and which he had, were becoming inhibiting because the company had evolved. We sat down and I said, 'We both know that this is not working any more.' It felt like the conversation at the end of an emotional relationship that had run into problems. We needed to agree, in a grown-up way, that things had changed and it was time to move on.

It's the same in personal relationships. In all relationships, both parties evolve naturally – ideally in the same direction and at the same rate – but if your personal evolution is not along the same path as that of your spouse or partner, or if one of you feels sidelined or bypassed by the other's evolution, therein lies potential unhappiness.

The relationship writer Paul Hudson says, 'We may not know exactly where our lives will take us and what we will learn – who we will become – along the way, but we can make a conscious effort to grow closer together and not apart.' He believes that most couples grow away from each other over the course of time because they believe they have done everything they need to do within their relationship. 'This is one of the main reasons marriages end up being so horrible – people think that there is no greater peak to climb than the one their relationship is already resting on. Marriage shouldn't be the end, it should be the beginning.'

If I was driving an emotional relationship with the same rate of change as I did in my work life, could my partner sustain the ability to evolve at the same pace? You can fall in love with someone and over time your persona, your aspirations and expectations, and your criteria of success and happiness change – and yet the person you are with has not changed, or indeed may have changed in a different direction. They are exactly the same person you fell in love with, but you have gone along different paths or perhaps at different speeds.

It is not her or his fault. That is exactly what happened with my ex-wife, Paola. She did nothing wrong. She is and was always lovely and yet I have gone on a different path and sought something else.

When you are at work for most of your waking hours, it is

hardly surprising that you can end up forming a relationship with someone in the same workplace; you are spending more time together than each of you are with your partners outside work.

If we consider it a necessity that we should be open to and aware of the risks associated with that, we should also be aware of the need to be flexible in our careers. Children leaving school are going to have an average of 14 jobs by the age of 38, as opposed to the old concept of a job for life. You can have a kind of monogamy (like my 13 years at TelecityGroup, or perhaps within one industry), but within that time your relationship must evolve multiple times.

## THE LIBERTY QUOTIENT

For me the departure from TelecityGroup signalled a period of significant liberation, the ability to talk to people about completely different industries, opportunities to move into areas of business that weren't available to me when I was limited to working within the data storage industry.

Pleasingly, people starting calling as soon as the news broke; a dozen calls on Day 1 from private equity guys, asking me if I could help take private companies public, and public companies private. This was a major boost to my self-confidence.

I learnt a few things. When I did go back into the office, some of the long-term staff would get a bit teary ('Oh Mike, it's not the same without you'), but a couple of those colleagues who I would have thought were going to be super loyal were not, when it came to the crunch, quite as loyal as I had anticipated. It was as if they were afraid of being too closely associated with me. As always happens, the board was trying to remove every trace of me, turning my old office into two meeting rooms, changing locks, the usual stuff. Some previously loyal staff understandably felt worried, put their heads down and didn't reply to my emails. I can understand that: everyone has their own agenda and a different tolerance of risk.

For my wife Shalina – who was overseeing the complete fit-out of our house, which happened to get under way at exactly this time – it was scary. I was choosing an independent career, starting my own business. 'You want to do this now?' she asked.

I had three months to plan before my last day in the company. Three months of runway before I had to fly solo. So I was technically continuing to work for the company while putting in place a structure to support my family and myself when that day came. I tried to set up a balance of clients who would be able to provide immediate short-term funding, and others where I could take a risk by agreeing a percentage of equity with the prospect of a slice of any exit the investors had five years down the line.

Meantime I was dismantling my previous life. As company CEO I had 38 directorships in 13 countries, so I had to resign from all those. Suddenly I couldn't even sign anyone's expenses. I had no responsibility within the company whatsoever, but the flipside was that my personal responsibility was extreme because I still had to get another job. It was liberating, but I was not entirely free, even though I could choose what I wanted to do. But being my own boss meant I could take my kids for breakfast on their birthdays. I was no longer at someone else's beck and call.

There was also an infrastructure to set up around myself.

It took me three attempts to get Windows on a Mac system to work without any tech support. Time was that I could have relied on my technical department to 'make it work'. Instead I spent hours on the phone with Apple and Microsoft sorting out private email addresses, and migrating emails across. I quickly had to create new company structures, branding, business cards, somewhere to base myself (the Arts Club in Mayfair turned out to be a wonderful central London 'office').

For the first time I could develop a proper social media presence. I had not really exploited Twitter before, because as the boss of a listed company I had to be extremely circumspect, since anything I said might have had a direct effect on share prices.

I rethought much of the way I had been operating. It was amazing how little I went into the City. Like most people I had thought that the City was where the money is: it's not. The City is where the *business* of money happens. But I came to realise that all the private equity companies were based in the West End.

I've learnt so much since I branched out on my own, not least about how I have had to rethink the impact my work has on the rest of my life.

## 45 DEGREES OF REALISATION

Having had the time to look back at my career and ahead to where I wanted to go, I saw that it would all be about finding a fresh angle on every aspect of my work and life.

We work flat out so much of the time that it is hard to find the space to reassess and plan. Just before a recent summer holiday, I received an email from the leadership specialist

Professor Colin Turner, who I had met at a TED talk, which summed this up perfectly: 'The best ideas are spawned outside the office: Einstein's relativity theory came to him while relaxing down on the grass away from the laboratory. The human mind does not require rest. It needs change of routine, environment and stimulus.' Colin's suggestion was to focus on a clear idea of what I wanted to achieve after the summer 'without concern as to how'. Then the holiday could be enjoyed. 'Your creative mind will reward you with the ideas you seek. Einstein imagined riding on a beam of light. [Steve] Jobs imagined 1000 songs in his pocket. Both changed the world.'

One of the difficulties of working and living is that neither can be perfect. Perhaps you can achieve success on one axis, at 0°, but screw up on the other axis, at 90°. Everyone I have ever known finds it excruciatingly difficult to avoid the clash between the two competing demands. I know from bitter experience that you will screw up on at least one objective if you try to achieve success on both.

So, I wondered, rather than trying to be perfect at 0° *and* 90°, maybe, just maybe, the ultimate is 45°. You can be 100 per cent on 45°.

The analogy I use is that you can't be an Olympic gold medal-winning weightlifter *and* a marathon runner. The muscles you need are completely different for each discipline. If you become supreme at one, it is probable that you will have to give up the other. If you enjoy both disciplines it is unlikely that you will be able to win a gold medal for *both*. However, you could train for the decathlon, which demands multiple talents.

A Paralympian like Richard Whitehead can't win the Olympic 200 metres with his artificial legs, but he can win the

Paralympic 200 metres (and, exceptionally, be a world champion in the marathon as well). The lack of his limbs does not prohibit him from achieving a different goal. Always looking at things from 45° is a good way of spotting the right opportunity.

You can ask yourself 'Am I the best salesperson?' and 'Am I the best parent?' but reconciling the two will always prove to be a dilemma. At work you might be the CEO. At home you are Dad or Mum.

A bunch of children were asked what they wanted for Christmas, and they all produced a list of want-to-haves, including the latest drones and must-have toys. Then they were given the choice between having their chosen present or having their parents at home for Christmas. Precisely 100 per cent of them said they would just want to spend time with their parents.

Children don't think in 45°. They are always 0° or 180°; there is rarely anything in between. If you are at home and stressed about something, they are unhappy. They don't know what your work entails, and why should they? But they will instinctively pick up on every aspect of your temperament.

If your family is at 0°, your work at 90°, you risk relationships at home going wrong. You're trying to juggle the impossible. It's never going to work until you find that 45° angle.

## THE REVOLUTIONARY ROAD – DYNAMIK ÜBER ALLES

The word 'disruption' in a business context is in danger of becoming a cliché. We need a new term for it. Its sense of a radical, revolutionary change to a long-established way of running a business or industry sector has become a rather lazy way of talking about any level of change, even if it is neither radical or revolutionary.

Disruption, usually seen as an interference, is now the norm. But 'norm' is a passive word. Let's see disruption as an opportunity, an invitation to make the most of constant transformation, to be continuously adaptable, to take advantage of the shifting tectonic plates of change.

Take Uber. Within a very short space of time – the company was founded in 2009 – the long-standing profession of cab and taxi drivers has been turned on its head, with a knock-on impact on other parts of the car industry. By 2016 Uber was worth more than Hertz, Avis and Europcar put together, and yet it did not own a single vehicle. It hadn't existed seven years before, but was already an everyday part, not only of our lives but of our language.

Once the car service was up and running, the company starting looking for other industries to which they could apply their mindset: UberEATS and UberFRESH for food delivery, taking their lead from companies like Deliveroo, and then AmazonFresh and Amazon Restaurants.

Travis Kalanick and Garrett Camp, the founders of Uber, changed the dynamic. That is the key word. Maybe rather than 'disruption' we need to say 'dynamisation' – somewhere between 'dynamic' and 'dynamite', exploding preconceptions, blowing up the stultified, old-school way of doing things.

Along the way the demographic of jobs has also shifted. When people express concern about technology destroying jobs, they have the wrong perspective. Technology moves jobs around. Traditional cab drivers may be in danger of losing their livelihoods, but Uber has hundreds of people writing the code for their services. It has thousands of drivers. Technology may not always create more jobs, but it does create different ones.

By developing this new business approach, Uber and its copycats may also have exploded their own futures. In five years' time Uber itself may well not exist: in due course, the drivers may themselves be replaced by driverless cars – a relatively short lifespan for an Uber driver.

Responsivity is the key. Kodak famously developed a digital photography system but couldn't industrialise it; they always thought there would be a space for proper film. After a century and more of existence, and as a byword for photography ('that Kodak moment'), they filed for Chapter 11 bankruptcy in 2012 – eventually re-emerging but drastically weakened and a fragment of their original self. They had the right vision but the wrong dynamic.

The trick is to 'Uber' yourself before someone else does. If as a business you can recognise the 'Uber' risk, you will be far more prepared for the threat. By creating an incubated entity within your own business, like developing a vaccine against fever, you can be brave enough to contemplate self-cannibalisation.

Of course, there is often no need for change. Management consultancies are always proposing change, because that proves that hiring them is worth the often sizeable fees they can command. They come in, listen to you tell them about your company, regurgitate everything they have heard back to you, say you need to make some changes, and then charge you for it. This is a classic way of generating change, but often the company is fundamentally sound and doing well, and doesn't actually need a new direction.

Nokia started life as a wood pulp mill company, was then an energy company, and at the turn of the twentieth century was manufacturing wellington boots. Later it produced car tyres, before moving into electronics, including televisions (remember the tiny ones in cheap hotels?), and then on to what our generation knows them for: mobile phones. Subsequently, it developed into a software company with the Symbian operating system and the Nokia brand as the world knew it virtually disappeared. Now it concentrates on licensing technologies to other manufacturers. I suggest that the principal reason for Nokia's downfall was the desire to create an independent software platform rather than sticking to the business of mobile phones they produced so well.

I am a proponent of responding to and provoking change where it is needed. But I have come to realise that there is also a time for preserving the status quo. Making the right choice around change is a key management skill.

## CHANGING PERCEPTIONS OF REALITY

I once invited a speaker to come in and talk to my management team about mental structures. One of the examples he used was as follows:

*Imagine you have left the office really late one winter's evening and are heading to the station to catch your train home. It is dark, quiet, there is no one around.*

*Along the way you have to turn down a small, badly lit alleyway. Halfway along it, you hear footsteps coming up behind you, and your immediate reaction is to think, 'What's that?' Danger flashes in your brain and suddenly the night seems darker and the alleyway longer. You speed up, but the footsteps behind you are also getting faster. Suddenly you are in full panic mode and start running. The footsteps run, too. You reach the station, out of breath, frazzled, turn round and find your pursuer is one of your colleagues. He doesn't normally get the train and, because he saw you speed up, he had thought the train was due to leave, so he started running too.*

*Now the reality was the reality. The reality did not change during that entire time. What did change was your response, because in your mind you had created an image of reality which was completely wrong. The scenario you imagined was perfectly possible, but it was wrong. And, of course, the moment you saw your colleague your worry dissipated immediately. All of that stress, that pain, that concern, was imaginary and nothing to do with reality.*

I came across a twist on this idea of perception and positive psychology at a recent TED talk. The speaker told us that when he was a young child and playing with his baby sister in a bunk bed, his sister fell off the bed onto the floor, landing on all fours. He could see she was just about to release this almighty howl and knew he was about to get into a ton of trouble with his parents, because he was supposed to be looking after her.

The only thing he could think to say was, 'Oh my goodness, you've landed on all fours. No normal human could land like that, you must be a magical unicorn,' knowing that the most wonderful thing on the planet for his sister would be to be a magical unicorn. He could see the cogs churning in her mind as she decided whether to go with pain and annoyance, or the delight she felt with the idea that she might just be a magical unicorn. She went for the latter and within seconds she was scuttling back up onto the top bunk, completely calm and happy. Again, the reality had not changed but, unwittingly, he had created an alternative perception of that reality.

The fact is that our perceptions (and preconceptions) can really get in the way of reality. We need to develop techniques to be able to respond differently to the situations in which we find ourselves, more innovatively, reimagining them in ways that will make a real difference. This will become ever more important as the world changes ever faster around us.

## TODAY'S TANGENTS, TOMORROW'S ARCS

There are people who can happily surf change, adjust their balance to stay upright as the swell beneath them fluctuates, who are seemingly unfazed by radical changes in their environment, circumstances or situation. That flexibility is something I wrote about in my previous book *Forget Strategy. Get Results*: the need to adapt or die, to stick to a crystal-clear vision but retain flexibility on the details. Such flexibility brings great value to life, and is perfectly attuned to the opportunities and possibilities of a web-connected world.

But that ability to flex, to flux, is a *response* to change. On top of that, an additional, vital skill is the ability to look at the way things are and imagine them differently, to create and prompt change by viewing the world through that 45° angle. Anyone who can do that is more likely to come up with new solutions, ideas that no one else has had before. In general, I have found it is entrepreneurs and innovators who possess that ability.

There is a theory that many entrepreneurs have a number of traits in common:

○ A significant **sense of abandonment or deprivation**, either due to a very poor upbringing (financial rather than emotional), a lack of a good or inspiring education, the absence of one or both parents. That becomes a key driver in their make-up, a deep desire to achieve security, love, respect and admiration. This in turn leads to a relentlessly obstinate, tenacious **determination and drive.**

○ **High energy levels** and a need – bordering on, if not tipping over into, ADD – to be constantly occupied and energised, invigorated and excited. Anything to avoid the horror of boredom.

○ Practicality and a **love of simple solutions**: acknowledging that the over complex gets in the way of achievement.

○ **Healthy egos,** but equally a strong sense of their weaknesses, which means they are happy to hire people to add in skills they do not themselves possess.

I'll leave it up to someone else to analyse me, but I can certainly identify with everything in that list.

I would also add one further item to the list: the skill of **looking at things at 45°.** This aligns with another identifiable entrepreneurial trait: non-conformity, that maverick wish to break the rules. The 90° or 180° route is far too predictable.

Head off at a tangent. Tangents are good. In fact, in a world that is, at one level, increasingly conforming, tangents are better than good: they are essential for survival.

# QR: AUGMENTED DISCOVERY

Click on the QR code at the end of this chapter. You'll instantly download clips of me telling you more about each of these key points:

- Looking at both work and life from a 45° angle may give us the perception to reimagine what we need to create to have satisfying and successful careers without sacrificing a fulfilling home life.

- You can't run a relationship like a spreadsheet, a to-do list or a strategy document. Relationships always evolve, but they don't necessarily have to change at the same pace as a business.

- Make sure that your evolution is broadly empathetic to, and in the same direction as, your partner's evolution; otherwise, the tension involved may tear the relationship apart.

- When, as will inevitably happen, your aspirations and expectations drift away from those of your partner, you need to invest time in being together, talking about any issues, understanding each other's change.

- We think of the world now as one of intense change and constant disruption, which can be quite frightening. But maybe we need to see this as a chance to achieve a genuinely positive transformation – for ourselves, our businesses and our loved ones.

*'Change will not come if we wait for some other person or some other time. We are the ones we've been waiting for. We are the change that we seek.'*

Barack Obama

Part II

# Part II

# LOVE

# Chapter 4

MT

LOVE ACTUALLY

# LOVE ACTUALLY

## Revaluing our relationships

*'To be successful you have to have your heart in your business and your business in your heart.'*

IBM CEO Thomas Watson Sr

A friend of mine once told me about his experience of starting work at Goldman Sachs. When graduate trainees like him landed their dream job at this legendary company and turned up – freshly scrubbed, bright-eyed and super keen – on their first day at work, they were promptly informed by their new mentors, as a key part of their induction process, that if they genuinely wanted to succeed within the company they should dump their current girlfriend or boyfriend – **immediately**.

The explanation given was that the huge, unrelenting workload and the high, if not stratospheric, standards expected of them would leave absolutely no time for any kind of emotional relationship. If they attempted to continue the relationship, it would, they were told, be doomed anyway: their partner would leave them in due course, because she or he would never see anything of them and would become frustrated and resentful.

Only after several years of training and focus would they finally be free to enjoy and nurture any kind of lasting relationship. It smacked of a monk-like indoctrination. Welcome to the company.

Is there a place for love in the workplace and business? Or is love a quality or a concept too intangible, too fickle and too volatile to co-exist with the sense of business as a structured, targeted, managed process? To many people it sounds slightly absurd even to think about placing 'love' into a business context.

It is true that love cannot be quantified in financial terms or entered into a field on a spreadsheet. Love is not hard data. Yet I firmly believe there is a role for love in business. Because business depends on relationships. And all the core aspects of love – truth, trust and commitment – apply just as much to business relationships as they do to personal ones.

Mandy O'Neill, assistant professor of management at George Mason University in Virginia, is a proponent of 'infusing' love into the workplace: what she terms 'companionate love'. She says that companionate love occurs in the relationships that make up the majority of our interactions:

*It involves affection, caring and compassion and has a much broader scope than romantic love: it can be experienced in the workplace, friendships and family relationships. In strong cultures of love, we observe that people care about one another's well-being, they look out for one another and pick up the slack for one another. A culture of love is not just something that takes place between two people, rather something that is pervasive throughout the organisation.*

When others have responded that love is not an appropriate emotion for the workplace, since it may dilute the necessary edge required in an achievement-orientated culture, she uses her research to counter the assumption that love is an opposite to competitiveness.

*We observed strong cultures of love in finance organisations – an industry that is as cut-throat as it gets in terms of competitiveness and aggressiveness. We found that the companionate love these very hard-working individuals feel for one another sustains their high levels of performance, with some putting in 17-hour days. When you care about your co-workers you're more motivated to work hard, put in the extra hours, because you like these people and they care about you as well.*

# LOVE: VALUE, INVESTMENT, RETURN

Value is never static. An orange, intact and unpeeled, simply a piece of fruit on sale in the supermarket, does not attract VAT. But cut it into pieces, place it into a juicer, liquefy, process (and essentially destroy) it, and lo and behold, suddenly it's VAT-able. Simply cutting it up and turning it into juice has given it, apparently, 'added value'.

When you are out shopping, there is a conundrum that constantly applies:

O The cheapest item may not be the best value.

O The most expensive item may not be the best value.

O The highest quality item may not be the best value.

It depends on your definition of 'value'.

The psychologist Oliver James talks about people seeing themselves and other people as commodities. Every day we go through a process of subliminally working out whether the people we come across are of value. You meet somebody and think, 'What can I get out of them? How do I make the most of this person?' rather than just allowing that person to be the person they are. In business, this means always seeking to maximise your relationship with someone else.

A commodity is essentially something you buy and then sell for more. That is the principle of an entrepreneur, a 'between taker': not the person who creates the value in the first place or the person who receives the value, but the person in the middle who brings these two together. But if you can set aside that mindset, maybe you can allow the value of something else to reveal itself: to allow the value of love to rise to the surface.

To take another commercial phrase, it is also possible to invest in love. Recently I travelled to Vienna to see my friend Anthony and take him out for lunch. Anthony is a brilliant artist and musician but, not untypically, he had often been out of work in the past. He was now experiencing another tough period. A few years previously I had two friends who had also gone through hard times and both ended up committing suicide. I only realised that I should have helped them when it was too late. I did not want the same thing to happen to Tony.

He was completely buzzed by the fact that I had taken the trouble to fly to Vienna specifically to see him. I was not there for business. I hadn't tagged our get-together on to the end of a board meeting. I was there for him. And I also asked him to do some work for me, work that I definitely needed and that I could pay him for: he would not have taken my money otherwise.

If you enter into a business relationship with an expectation of failure, disappointment or of suspicion, you will probably prove yourself to be right. But if you start any relationship expecting the best and are prepared (but hoping not) to be proved otherwise, you can at least see where events will lead. That investment in love frequently leads to a far greater return.

The first time I went to an interview with the computing company ICL, I was running very late, painfully and embarrassingly late, due to a series of traffic hold-ups. I arrived at ICL's offices frustrated and hassled. Peter Long, the company's HR director, welcomed me to the interview by immediately putting me at ease. 'We were sitting here,' he mused, 'thinking how stressful it must have been for you to be held up coming to an interview, so I want you to know it doesn't affect your chance of getting this job in the slightest.' He had placed himself in my shoes. And it endeared him to me. At that point he was the sole embodiment of ICL that I had encountered, so I felt wanted, comfortable, loved. And naturally I also felt like this was a company I really wanted to work for.

## RELATIONSHIPS WITHIN WORK

*'Love should be treated like a business deal, but every business deal has its own terms and its own currency. And in love, the currency is virtue.'*

Ayn Rand

Relationships with colleagues and contacts at work can easily interfere with relationships *outside* work. Anyone who has experienced leaving home at 7 am to commute, painfully, on the train into work will know the feeling of returning twelve or more hours later to discover a family already winding down for sleep.

There may only be an hour or so, maybe even less, available

for shared family time. And that time may well not be quality time: the kids cranky after having had to finish their homework or do their piano practice, or fixated on their tablets and phones, a partner who is exhausted from co-ordinating all the family activities and who is not in the mood for a chat about just how great, or problematic, your own day was.

Meanwhile, you spend the vast majority of your active, waking time with people at work in an environment which often offers – in a successful company – a huge amount of positive energy, along with shared risks and confidences.

When being at home seems like a depressing chore, it is small wonder that office affairs happen. And if you are successful at work, that confidence boosts your attractiveness, especially if a partner at home doesn't seem to find you that attractive any more (or more likely is just too exhausted to tell you that they do), and the likelihood of something being triggered at the office increases.

Work affairs are not usually a good thing (although sometimes those relationships can evolve and endure) and are often simply a short-term fix to a much deeper core problem. The question is: what is the value of those relationships? I know this only too well, because I have been there.

I had the experience of stressful times, bringing up young kids while working in a demanding job. The last thing I wanted to do was carry on discussing work at home. I wanted to escape. It was far easier to build alliances and relationships with people at work than at home, to find what I perceived as sympathy and empathy. At work, people understood and related to the same issues, without me having to explain all the details.

Add into that mix a lack of self-belief, plus a wanting and

needing to be loved, and there were all the ingredients for the beginning of the destruction of my marriage. There were of course many other factors, but the fact that I drew a clear distinction between work and home, whether I was conditioned or forced to, was the single biggest reason that I failed in my personal life.

The moment I separated from my family is almost too painful to recall, but the atmosphere in the house had grown so bad I didn't know where the future was. Doing something radical, knowing that in the long term it was for the best, was the only solution.

This book is not necessarily meant to be a personal confessional, although one of the starting points for writing it was my reflecting about some of the things I have done wrong in my life. I am happy to be open about the screw-ups I've made, but the more I thought about it, and talked about it, the more I discovered that these fault lines were very common among people who have achieved success. Friends and colleagues immediately related to the issue of trying to hold on to a relationship at home as well as succeeding at work.

## LOVE AT WORK, LOVE AT HOME

Part of the problem is that we tend to behave differently at work. When I was at Telecity, if there was an external interruption from a colleague while I was holding a meeting in my office, I would politely ask the others in the meeting to excuse me for a few minutes while I found out what the problem was. Or I might ask my colleague if I could get back to them in half an hour once the meeting was over. It was all very civilised, manageable, professional.

At home, on the other hand, I might be having the equivalent of my 'meeting' – with my computer, or the TV – with the kids in the other room making a noise, and one of them shouting, 'Daddy, Daddy', having a meltdown. In the past, I would probably have shouted back irritably, 'For God's sake, bugger off, I'm busy...' Now, why wouldn't I treat my kids with the same respect I showed my colleagues? Was it because at work I was being paid to deal with issues, to solve problems, and at home the same rules didn't apply?

This is one of the dilemmas of a clear work/life divide: a business person, who has a certain level of status, prestige or respect at work, is simply Mum, Dad, a husband, wife or partner at home.

This work/home differential can ruthlessly destroy family relationships (the work side seems to suffer less), simply because of the perceived need to create a distinction between them. With ever greater pressure on people to succeed, we are forced to decide between work and life more and more, and the challenge and struggle of achieving the perfect 'balance' drives a wedge between the two.

This goes back to the question of value and self-worth in a relationship, and why there can be a sense of alienation at home, in the very place where you should be able to relax and soothe away the stresses of work. Anyone who feels undervalued at home has the potential to become resentful, with a festering silent aggression creating more tension.

Work also provides a role, a job with a title (however meaningless). As human beings we seem to like being labelled, having our roles defined. If you work in a restaurant, you might be a chef or a sous-chef; the maître d' or a waiter. But at home you fulfil many, often ill-defined and overlapping, roles:

parent, cook, nurse, tutor, chauffeur. At home there are many roles with far less definition or status attached to them.

Why would a successful business person want to sit at home and care for a toddler, if he or she thinks that means not being the breadwinner? Well, that is already the start of the problem, because you need to keep in mind what you are winning the bread for: your family.

The major stakeholder in you is your family. They have a vested interest in your existence, your well-being, your success and your happiness. And, as your major stakeholder, if you are completely screwing everything up at home, is it any wonder that, ultimately, being 'fired' is an option?

Equally, if one partner is the primary care-provider, they feel their worth drop, even though the role of houseparent is critical. Before kids they might have been a high flyer. Now they are 'just' a mother or father, being moaned at by all and sundry, with few accolades and precious little recognition, perceived as a dull stay-at-home. Naturally their self-worth is affected.

## DON'T DILUTE THE VALUE OF LOVE

In the 1960s, 40 per cent of women were prepared to marry a man if everything else was right about him but they didn't actually love him. That percentage had dropped to 15 per cent of women by the 1990s. At the same time, the divorce rate has increased significantly. Although everyone knows there is a premium on love, that premium is not always being applied in practice.

Only when you truly integrate life and work do you get the full value of being loved, and of loving. It is extremely difficult to love many people, and to be loved by many: it requires focus, energy and a big heart. Too often the last element is missing.

A large swathe of people, men in particular, see love as a game or a challenge, all about the winning and the conquering. In the past I had many relationships that did not eventually work, even though the other person loved me. The problem was that at the moment they loved me, I was done. I had won. I left a trail of emotional destruction behind me. Most of the time, when I went into those relationships I would honestly be in love, or what I thought being in love meant, but when the love was given back to me I moved on.

I never quenched my thirst for being loved because, each time a new norm was achieved, I needed something more again. I wanted to prove to myself that I was still wanted, still desirable. And, to my shame, I realise I thought of many of those conquests as a commodity. Needless to say, this does not make me proud.

During one of the biggest deals of my career, I had a relationship with the PA of the head of the private equity house representing the other side, for no other reason than to glean useful information. I could not have known whether she would be damaged by the relationship or not. And, quite frankly, I didn't care.

Worse than this, there was one point when I was in a relationship with four women at the same time, and was blind copying them the same text messages. Needless to say, one day I accidentally cc'd them all instead of bcc'ing them. They all arranged to get their revenge. One of them arranged to meet me for a drink. When I arrived, all the others were sitting there as well. The reception I got served me right.

If you have true love in a relationship, you are bound by

trust, by choice. Instead of being in each other's pocket, you feel liberated.

In the past, due to my selfishness, I have hurt many people with whom I have been in personal relationships, but I am grateful for now being able to see that, and for understanding that mistakes are simply learning experiences which, once understood, become valuable.

## CALLING TIME ON A RELATIONSHIP

Just as personal relationships depend on happiness, so too do relationships in business. If a partnership has soured, and is becoming detrimental to progress, then it may be the right point to call time on the relationship, however successful or valuable it appears on the surface.

If any relationship is built on dodgy foundations, then the edifice above will collapse – maybe not this year, maybe not next year, but inevitably at some point in the future. Just as we have to be prepared to be brave and to create a new personal relationship if an older one has withered, the same applies at work. We are always involved in constantly changing relationships, whether emotional or business ones. The essential thing is that we continue to evolve throughout our personal relationships, throughout a marriage, throughout our career.

Another contributing factor to the break-up of my first marriage was the fact that I was living with my family in the Kent countryside and travelling to London or abroad, staying away for substantial chunks of time. That certainly made home life more difficult and, from my ex-wife's point of view, lopsided in terms of my input to our three children's daily life.

Now I am living in London, which is a more expensive

solution, but one which is better for a relationship since I spend less time commuting. I have also limited my travelling, and try to complete European trips within one or at most two days if at all possible. If the trip has to be longer because it is further away, then Shalina often chooses to come along with me. I am more comfortable with Shalina going out or travelling by herself. This used to be an issue for me, which was my problem: I needed to be in control of everything, my success and my partner included.

Defensiveness comes from insecurity, and insecurity comes from a feeling of inadequacy. The love you feel as a child comes from the knowledge that you are going to be fed, bathed, put into bed: that creates a security that breeds confidence. A lack of security delivers a negative impact in later life.

Oliver James explains that children who are abused or uncared for at a very young age have a significantly smaller hippocampus; there is a physical change in their brain. Different parts of the brain grow at different rates according to whether people are well loved. It is not impossible, but very difficult, to fix.

I enjoy studying my fellow business travellers doing their best to love and care for their kids, from wherever they are on the planet. FaceTiming their kids at their bedtime in a different time zone, and showing them around with the phone or iPad. How awesome is that? Their kids get a real-time explanation of a land which is far away and, contrary to feeling distant from a parent who normally tucks them into bed, they can look forward to this live video adventure just as they would a bedtime story. I have peeked over the shoulder of these fathers and mothers, and been struck by the wonder in their child's eye when seeing a Tokyo scene through Skype and being told about the magic of the faraway city, being narrated *live* by their dad or their mum at bedtime. Technology, yet again, adds rather than subtracts, multiplies rather than divides.

# LEARNING HOW TO LOVE YOURSELF

A few months ago I was holding a meeting with the head of a business I am involved in, a good business but one operating in a very challenging environment. We were trying to identify which aspects of the business were working well and which were problematic, and where to focus on making improvements.

Every time I made a suggestion about an adjustment or proposed sending someone on a training programme, the MD always started his reply with the same phrase: 'The problem with that is…' This happened half a dozen times and it occurred to me that it was his defensive position. I was sure he had not reflected on any of this in advance. It was his default, knee-jerk response, because he took my suggestions as criticism. He thought he was being judged. I was just trying to help him achieve more.

Within a family environment we are constantly saying to our children, 'Don't do this' or 'Stop doing that'. Much of the time this is because we love them and don't want them to get hurt or fail in something. They see it as interference. Maybe there's an analogy there. Our perception of love often differs from that of the recipient.

Part of being able to love other people is being able to love yourself. If you are in a position to love yourself, if you are comfortable in your own skin, you give yourself more leeway to love other people.

That is why I am so certain that by dispensing with the

outdated concept of work/life balance and replacing it with work/life integration, we have a chance of succeeding at our whole lives instead of just one part of it.

## LISTEN TO YOUR HEART

Your heart is a powerful resource. We tend to think that the brain is where all the decision-making is focused. But, while the brain does have an electromagnetic field, it is, in fact, relatively weak compared to the heart. The heart generates the largest electromagnetic field within our bodies, approximately 60 times greater in amplitude than that of brainwaves recorded in an electroencephalogram (EEG).

Physics now tells us that if we can change either the electric or magnetic field of an atom, we are able to change that atom and its elements within our body. The human heart is designed to do that – and perhaps that's why the quality of love can fluctuate too.

So, to extend the analogy, make the most of your own heart, the love you can bring to both home and work life. By being open and flexible and following your heart, nurturing love at home and bringing it into the workplace, you'll find that you are better able to weather storms on both fronts. This is the power of embracing the idea of work/life integration.

## QR: AUGMENTED DISCOVERY

Click on the QR code at the end of this chapter. You'll instantly download clips of me telling you more about each of these key points:

■ Business depends, utterly and completely, on relationships. Trust, integrity, honesty, truth, commitment, openness: exactly the same elements that hold a personal relationship together, and the absence of which can blow one apart.

■ Learn when to be honest with yourself and draw a line under a relationship that is proving to be destructive and detrimental. What might once have been a positive and profitable relationship may now be dragging you down.

■ Put the pro in professional, not the con in confrontational.

■ If you can't find an equilibrium between your home and work life, one element is bound to suffer. So rethink the whole equation: work and life can be integrated, to the benefit of both.

■ Define yourself by what you love, not by what you don't. Be pro things, not automatically anti.

■ Don't rush and don't panic. Very little in life goes to plan. That's why I called my first book *Forget Strategy. Get Results*.

*'Some things don't matter much; like the colour of a house; how big is that in the overall scheme of life? But lifting a person's heart: now, that matters. The whole problem with people is they know what matters, but they don't choose it. The hardest thing on earth is choosing what matters.'*

Sue Monk Kidd

# Chapter 5

MT

LOVE UNEQUIVOCALLY

# LOVE UNEQUIVOCALLY

## Delivering love with vision and humility

*'I always wanted to tell a story about Abraham Lincoln.
I saw a paternal father figure; I saw someone who was
completely, stubbornly committed to his ideas, to his vision.'*

Steven Spielberg

The role of the business leader has a lot in common with being the leader of a family. There can be plenty of misunderstandings, feuds and brooding resentment – but equally that paterfamilias or materfamilias role can infuse the whole of the family/company with purpose and vision. That's the upside of a top-down structure (we'll come to the downside later).

Poll a selection of business managers for the names of great CEOs, and Richard Branson, Bill Gates and Steve Jobs will almost always be in the list, alongside Larry Ellison of Oracle. One of Larry Ellison's employees once described their boss in these terms: 'The difference between God and Larry is that God does not believe he is Larry.'

Ask a group of voters for the names of great political leaders and the names of J. F. Kennedy, Nelson Mandela,

Winston S. Churchill and Bill Clinton will inevitably come up.

As well as dominant political or business figures, all of these leaders are also considered to be narcissists (intriguingly, no women appear on any of these narcissist lists, though perhaps Margaret Thatcher might qualify). And, inspirational though they were, Clinton, Mandela and JFK were all completely useless in their home lives. Is there a trend here?

At dinner a couple of years ago a fellow CEO asked me, 'Do we just *act* being CEOs?' He went on to explain that when he got back home each evening, his kids were always shouting 'Daddy, Daddy', wanting a bit of his time. Do we go home for a rest, to say, 'I had such a bad day at work, don't bug me, this is my down time?' His point was: why is your home time your down time? Isn't that what we are all actually working towards, to have a good home life? And yet, are we losing all of that because we are using it as our down time from work? Are we *acting* as CEOs, like an actor walks on the stage, putting up a pretence, a façade? Or perhaps, even more worryingly, our true selves are at work and our home life is the fake? Maybe that is the answer to why so many successful people fail at home: they are acting.

In January 2017, one narcissistic leader who – perhaps for the first time ever – straddled both the business and political arenas at the highest level was inaugurated as the 45th President of the United States: Donald J. Trump.

The narcissistic personality type was identified by the legendary psychoanalyst Sigmund Freud, who characterised the type as arrogant, with a sense of entitlement, assertive and highly goal-driven. Narcissists are self-absorbed, enjoy being the centre of attention, are visionary and bold risk-takers.

They attract followers because of their 'magnetic personality'. In fact, Freud wrote: 'People of this type impress others as being "personalities". Their charisma, itself a product of their unwavering self-belief, is one of the reasons so many narcissists "get away with it".' These leaders also have a co-dependent relationship with their followers. Narcissistic leaders need their followers, but those followers also look up to their leaders for a sense of security and a sense of their place in the hierarchy.

Perhaps surprisingly, Mahatma Gandhi's name also crops up in some lists of narcissistic leaders, along with a suggestion that he must have had an incredible sense of self-importance to believe that the British government would care if he chose to starve himself to death.

Others see Gandhi as more of a charismatic leader, forceful but caring deeply about others, whereas narcissists don't really care whether anyone gets trampled along the way in their desire to achieve their aims. However, a recent Gandhi biography claimed that he was a wife-beater, racist and slept with underage girls. True or not, that underlines the fact that all leaders – all people, come to that – are complex, complicated mechanisms whose true character cannot be summed up simply either by a hagiography or in a tabloid or Twitter smear.

Bart Wille, an assistant professor in personnel and organisational development at Ghent University, led a team who produced a report looking at how 'aberrant personality tendencies are associated with career and financial success'. This was based on following 250 alumni over 15 years, using a specific personality inventory (the NEO PI-R). Among their findings were that aberrant personality tendencies were very stable across that time period. Those with antisocial and narcissistic characteristics, they found, tended to rise higher in their careers and make the most money.

The research outlines the advantages of being slightly crazy for career success. Management consultant Ken Nowack analysed Bart Wille's research. He reinforced the report's conclusion that these 'organisational psychopaths' were generally more highly motivated, more politically savvy and more seriously competitive than other leaders, and therefore more likely to rise up through the strata of an organisation:

*They are more motivated because they are turned on by power and prestige. They are equipped for career success because they lack a genuine concern for others, are ruthless at times and prepared to lie to get what they want, and typically present a charming façade and appear to be an ideal leader (at least initially). These results are interesting in light of several findings suggesting that narcissistic leaders might rise in organisations but they are certainly not valued.*

There's that 'value' word again. So how do we make sure that leaders create long-term value both at work and at home?

## PRIVATE AND PUBLIC

Most people I talk to agree about the balance or, more accurately, the disconnect, between private and public personas for leaders. Successful business leaders at work are often complete screw-ups in their family lives. Clinton and Kennedy alone have generated millions of words of analysis on exactly that point.

The inability to articulate the difference between family and work is one of the reasons why family businesses often fail to make good business decisions: family love or family resentments get in the way. This is because there is no discipline in the integration. One has to embrace and integrate work and life without compromising clarity of vision in both cases.

I worked with a family company that involved two male siblings and a third non-family director. The two brothers were driving the business into the ground because they were wasting significant amounts of time and effort whingeing about each other: each brother about the other, and the two brothers jointly about the third director, with the mum stepping in and moaning about the whole lot of them. I was brought in because they wanted somebody who had no axe to grind.

What is clear is that people see business and family as separate entities. So, if there is a family event in the diary, most people have little compunction about cancelling it at the last minute with some excuse or other, or just turning up late, whereas they would – if you asked them – swear that they were never late for a business appointment, which might be true. Is the threat of being dismissed at work greater than the fear of being 'dismissed' at home?

Both families and businesses are tender beings that require a healthy dose of TLC to flourish. We need to ask ourselves, 'How can business leaders who automatically tend towards nourishing their businesses also make the same contribution to a flourishing family?'

## PATER AND MATERFAMILIAS

Naomi Shragai, writing in the *Financial Times* about 'Why we see bosses as parents', observed that 'executives in particular can find themselves on the receiving end of a host of strong feelings that their staff bring to work'. Manfred Kets de Vries, a psychoanalyst and professor in leadership development and organisational change at INSEAD business school, has written about this extensively. He describes how workers can respond to their leaders as they would have done to their parents or other authority figures while growing up:

*Executives can become a kind of emotional dumping ground for people's unresolved feelings and desires. The reaction they provoke can be both extremely positive or extremely negative, and frequently flips from one to another.*

As Naomi Shragai puts it, 'It is an unfortunate fact that we cannot run and hide from our dysfunctional families – but we can learn to keep them out of the office.'

This is the traditional view of the boss as parent. The same values apply to the paterfamilias or materfamilias, whoever is the 'leader' of a family. Little wonder that leaders have a tendency to exhibit these 'parenting'-type behaviours outside the home, especially as those qualities that make us successful at home also apply at work:

O Great leaders are who they say they are, and possess exemplary integrity.

O Vulnerability and humility are the hallmarks of an authentic leader, characteristics which create a positive, attractive energy.

O Customers, employees and media tend to want to help an authentic person to succeed.

My thinking is that, rather than trying to separate how we are at work from how we are at home, we should embrace these common characteristics and ensure we use them to the full wherever we are.

The social internet is also changing the divide between the public self and private self. Tomorrow's leaders necessarily have to be transparent about who they are, whether that is online or in person, merging their personal and professional lives together.

How many late-night Tweets or alcohol-induced emails full of aggression and exclamation marks have we all sent? They leave behind a permanent digital footprint. However rueful we are after sending them, the evidence persists. We could all do well to download the app that allows you to enter certain contact numbers and actively prevents, or at least checks, you from texting an ex after midnight.

I was out late at an event a few months ago, and ended up having a row with my wife. I had to get up super early the next morning to fly to Berlin, and the row was unresolved. I sent her a couple of chilly texts; she sent me a couple of equally chilly texts back. I was giving the keynote address at an event in Potsdam, arrived there after an hour in the car from the airport, and the first thing I had to do was sign 200 books for everyone who was attending.

I was signing each one 'Best regards', and every single time as I opened the book up I saw the dedication, which read, 'To my wife Shalina, whose "leap of faith" has given me happiness beyond measure.' So I texted her mid-signing to say, 'I am actually stopping now, because this is ridiculous. I am trying to be angry with you and I am seeing this message 200 times, every time I open this bloody book.' And she said, 'OK, I am sorry as well.'

We humans are inherently a bit lazy, forgetting phone numbers because it's easier to rely on digital contact lists, and allowing predictive texts to screw us up because we can't be bothered to check what we've actually written. As ever, it depends on how and why you use technology. I bought the

Amazon Echo set-up for my home. I already had the ability to open the curtains up at home wherever I was in the world, but now, with the words 'Hey Alexa, can you open the curtains for me?' I don't even need an app, I can voice-activate almost anything at home.

However, we shouldn't use these shortcuts with relationships, whether we're at home or at work. Great leaders may, in the past, have focused on their work relationships to the detriment of those at home. Improved connectivity should allow us to give the same level of attention and nurturing to our families too.

## INVERTING THE HIERARCHY – CREATING A LOWER-ARCHY

We can also learn at work from the positive relationships we forge and the behaviours we show at home. Many companies still operate in a traditional top-down bureaucratic way that means the vast majority of employees never have any relevant contact with the person who is making the decisions that directly affect them, or any understanding of why those decisions are made.

I would like to propose an alternative viewpoint. Business leaders need to have a role that, rather than reinforcing hierarchy, demands authenticity and a nurturing instinct.

A friend of mine was working for J. P. Morgan. While he was flying high at the company, his wife, although far from being a stay-at-home mum, had taken a local job that hardly stimulated her – and they weren't getting on that well. But then she began working as an assistant for a senior British politician who had stepped down from an active role in UK politics, helping him on his charity activities, humanitarian work and overseas trips. And at the same time, as her job became more interesting and stimulating for her, she and her husband's own relationship picked up. She might call to ask him if he could get home a bit earlier to pick up their kids from after-school clubs, whereas before she would always have done that. They found they were working more closely as a team; the old bread-winner vs homemaker division had been eradicated and their relationship was far better because of it. Involving people and promoting teamwork at work – at all levels of an organisation – can have a similarly positive effect.

The Mafia is perhaps the ultimate family business, and at the heart of it sits the Don. I'm not necessarily sure that Don Corleone is the business model we want to follow, or I wish to propose, but within that word 'Don' is a sense of donnishness – of wisdom and experience. And of donning and doffing the cap, of assuming responsibility while also respecting others. And, essentially, the idea that looking after the family is good for business.

Another interesting trend with regard to work/life integration is the rise of 'homepreneurship'. The UK currently has nearly 3 million home-based businesses, some of which have traded on that very quality, like Not On The High Street. It's a sector of industry that contributes something in the region of £300 billion to the UK economy each year: a tribute to keeping start-up costs low and making the most of sales opportunities by using technology and social media as a core marketing, sales and PR tool. Initially, homepreneurs were based in the creative sector, as design studios and magazine and book publishers found it was easier, and more cost-effective, to outsource their work. But, increasingly, companies based at home are offering business services, including consulting in law, science, accountancy, engineering and IT. What better example of the lower-archy and the inversion of traditional work models.

## INSTAGRAM HUSBANDS, RABBITS AND MONKEYS

Personal relationships are in a state of flux and, in many cases, our home roles are becoming semi-professionalised. Take Instagram husbands. Because people are uploading huge numbers of images to Instagram – Kim Kardashian took a four-day trip to Ibiza and posted 6,000 pictures of herself on Instagram – everyone is looking for the perfect yoga pose or pout. And it falls to the Instagram husband – who doesn't necessarily have to be male – to take that picture. Wives have turned their husbands or significant others, male or female, into personal photographers, human selfie sticks.

The phenomenon of the Instagram husband was explored by Kasmira Gander in the *Independent*.

*They say that behind every great man is a great woman, but an updated version of that saying might go: 'behind every flawless street-style Instagram photo is an exhausted photographer breaking their back to get the perfect angle'. That is the life of the so-called Instagram husband – those poor unrecognised people behind stunning Instagram accounts … Businesses have also seized upon the phenomenon, with Task Rabbit recently offering Instagram Husband and Wifey services during New York Fashion Week. And snaps of Kanye West and Jay-Z taking photos of Kim Kardashian and Beyoncé have shown that anyone can be a victim.*

'It also goes to show that no matter how big you are, you'll still need to be a good Instagram husband occasionally,' says Jeff Houghton, a TV presenter who lives in Springfield, in the US state of Missouri, and is among the most famous of Instagram husbands. He lives with his wife Michelle Houghton, who is a school counsellor and has over 3,000 followers on the app. 'An Instagram husband refers to anybody who has to begrudgingly take pictures of their significant other,' explains Jeff.

Closely related is the task rabbit, a more official Instagram husband with a job title and salary. The task rabbit – a temporary personal assistant or gopher – will be booked to help you move house, hang photos, carry your gift bags, handle your sample returns, all things that might have been handled more informally in the past.

Don't confuse them with chaos monkeys: imagine a chimpanzee rampaging through a data centre powering everything from Google to Facebook. Infrastructure engineers use a software version of this 'chaos monkey' to test the robustness of online services – their ability to survive random failure and correct mistakes before they actually occur. Tech entrepreneurs are society's chaos monkeys, disrupters testing and transforming every aspect of contemporary lives, from transportation (Uber) and lodging (Airbnb) to television (Netflix) and dating (Tinder).

I prefer to think of our roles within the family as that of shareholders, or stakeholders. We all have a boss, but we can call them different things. Instead of pigeonholing the leader as a dictator (or pigeonholing your partner as an Instagram husband), consider them, as we all are, as a stakeholder who has a vested interest in your performance. If you don't perform, they can't deliver. Within a company there are many stakeholders, including your peers – if you let them down, if you don't perform, maybe they won't get a group bonus. The same applies at home.

The biggest stakeholding you have is within your family, who are relying on you not just financially but also emotionally. If you come back home at the end of a long day and say, 'I didn't get paid today,' that creates an immediate problem, but it's also a problem if you are unable to invest in them emotionally too.

## NURTURING THE CREATOR

I believe that the business leader needs to care about and nurture the creators within their organisation.

Creators are not business people. They do not display the bravado, balls and braggadocio of the panel on a show like *Dragons' Den*. Those people are investors, not creators.

Creators in a business are delicate people. They are like painters. Painters don't as a rule – unless they are Lucien Freud or Damien Hirst – make money. Painters make art, and the people around painters make a shedload of money.

Entrepreneurs are creative enablers. It is rare that you find a blend of business and inventive creativity coming together in one person, which is why teams are important, bringing together people with different skills.

This role for a business leader is like nurturing your children or grandchildren. Entrepreneurs (or, at least, the true breed of entrepreneurs) are not people who rise up the ranks and become CEOs. They are mavericks, round pegs in the square holes, people who don't abide by social norms or easily fit into large groups, be it social groups or corporations. Most exceptional entrepreneurs are terrible leaders. So leaders can't rely on the entrepreneurs to look after the creators.

## LOOK FOR THE ENTREPRENEURS AROUND YOU

If you can liberate people to get rid of their fear of failure, they will go off to deliver, with no management involved, with no old-school leadership. People build their own routes and directions, and they grow as people, not just as employees.

We tend to train people only in the role they currently fulfil. But, if you are an engineer, why not go off and complete an MBA (or vice versa)? That is why an apprenticeship, which I took after leaving school, is so valuable. You get to see every aspect of a business, from production to sales to quality control; how the whole enterprise meshes together. The word 'apprentice' comes from the French 'apprendre', to learn. Take that opportunity with both hands.

Similarly, when I was at TelecityGroup, I gave the 16-strong management team the chance to take a residential course at a range of major business schools, including Oxford, INSEAD and Wharton. The courses would last up to six weeks. Normally no one would think they could take six weeks out of their annual schedule, but, because I insisted, they did. At least half of them moved up to higher positions following their time on the course.

I spoke to one of them recently, now working in Sweden: he had struck a deal as a direct result of meeting someone at an Oxford course, and whom he re-met at an alumni event. He said that the confidence he had from attending the course had helped him up his game, and he felt able to talk to somebody more senior than him. The result – a change of job, with new and greater responsibilities.

## AUTHENTIC LEADERSHIP

*'I had no idea that being your authentic self could make me as rich as I've become. If I had, I'd have done it a lot earlier.'*

Oprah Winfrey

Leadership skills are rarely taught – however many books, blogs and articles claim to contain the secret. The general assumption is that we acquire those skills in time and by doing. The reality is that the breadth of people skills that being a leader requires needs conscious, constant effort. And, if you stay true to your vision, you will find that effort and the solutions required far easier to come by. Great leadership is the single most important quality any entity, business or personal, needs to succeed. Ralph Nader famously observed that 'the function of leadership is to produce more leaders'.

Nobody cares about what you believe in unless they believe that you care. If you are a passionate leader, and genuinely want the best for your staff – exhibiting charisma rather than narcissism – they will follow and listen to you more.

*Raconteur* magazine reported on the use of technology to test staff commitment. Monica Parker, an organisational behaviouralist and social scientist at management consultancy Morgan Lovell, said 'Human beings are complicated creatures. When it comes to measuring their engagement, it's simply not enough to ask them, "Are you happy?" or "Are we, as your employer, giving you what you want?"'

'The view that employee engagement or its effects on

company performance can't be measured is pretty outdated,' says Laurence Collins, director of HR and workforce analytics at management consultancy Deloitte. The real watershed moment, he says, came as far back as 1998, with the publication of a study in the *Harvard Business Review*, showing how US retailer Sears was able to reverse its previously poor financial performance by improving employee engagement. 'That made a lot of human resources professionals sit up and take notice,' says Collins. For smart companies, the interaction of employees with technology can provide a rich source of data about their levels of engagement. But technology isn't just a source of data for gauging employee engagement. 'Technology is essential to keeping today's global workforce engaged,' says Forrester analyst T. J. Kett. 'Ideation tools, performance management software, gamification, social collaboration tools and mobile devices are just a few of the elements of a growing toolkit that keeps employees engaged, productive and focused on having a positive impact on customers.'

Perhaps the perfect inverse of this is the oDesk or Upwork example. In a typical open-plan office structure, staff work behind screens, in cubicles or pods. The oDesk software is designed for companies in which most people work from home, reflecting the changes in styles of employment. If you sign up to this system, you agree to your home laptop running a real-time camera.

Your boss (like a teacher in an old-style language lab) is able to listen in, and watch you at any point to see if you are actively working or playing Candy Crush. Not only can he or she monitor you through the computer screen, but the system can detect and report back on the actual keystrokes you are making, so you can't just look busy – it's a bit like that old one-liner 'Jesus is coming, look busy'. But does that level of surveillance actually work? Does *quantity* of output equal *quality* of output?

If I had been writing this book, and this chapter in particular, twenty or even ten years ago, I would probably have been on the side of the narcissist, confidently espousing the whole Gordon Gekko creed of 'greed is good'. Well, times change, and I have come to see that engagement at work is the equivalent of love at home. Both create trust and long-term value. People are the heart of a family, and the soul of a business.

# QR: AUGMENTED DISCOVERY

Click on the QR code at the end of this chapter. You'll instantly download clips of me telling you more about each of these key points:

- Good business leadership has much in common with being the patriarch or matriarch of a family – leaders who are arrogant, driven or assertive collect followers, but usually work best in the short term, not over a lifetime.

- In business, that kind of leader can offer a strong public profile, especially in the current era of soundbites and recognisability. But below them many employees feel disenfranchised.

- Much better for business leaders to, yes, lead (someone has to take the final decision and let the buck stop with them), but also to nurture the whole company, through showing vulnerability, humility and authenticity.

- Find the entrepreneurs who work for and with you; they need space to grow. They are often dreadful managers but inspiring colleagues, and – given the time to evolve – fantastic leaders.

- ■ Authentic leadership is about finding ways to engage employees, treating them with respect and consideration and sharing your vision with them.

> *'If you hire people just because they can do a job, they'll work for your money. But if you hire people who believe what you believe, they'll work for you with blood and sweat and tears.'*
>
> Simon Sinek

# Chapter 6

# LOVE WITH ALL YOUR HEART

## Overcoming conflict

*'There is an immutable conflict at work, in life and in business, a constant battle between peace and chaos.'*

Nike founder Philip Knight

Like all families, all businesses contain the element of conflict. The key is how you choose to deal with it.

Conflict is increasingly a part of work and home life. We feel under pressure, under scrutiny, under the cosh. I have seen this in the companies I have worked for or been involved in. Increasingly, staff are constrained in the way they are allowed to operate. The business may still be successful but the environment may not be conducive to collaboration.

I knew it was time to move on from TelecityGroup when meetings were being convened to discuss the tiniest, most mundane of administration details and team members found themselves disenfranchised and disempowered, especially when they realised that the top level of management or the company's owners did not care about them as individuals. They became unhappy, and that unhappiness sooner or later spilled over into a lack of tolerance, a lack of leeway and the build-up of conflict.

# HERDING CATS, MARSHALLING FORCES

*'When dealing with people, remember you are not dealing with creatures of logic, but creatures of emotion.'*

Dale Carnegie

Within any business, you'll find elements of an extended family:

O The young ones, apprentices/new employees who are learning. I am a huge supporter of apprenticeships, and a believer in nurturing those who are new to a business environment and who – with the vision to progress – have immense capacity and potential for development.

O Siblings and their rivalries, with the inevitable battles as opportunities for progress diminish. Even if there is no old-style Christmas-tree organigram structure, the quest to succeed can pitch members into a feud.

O Black sheep. The key is to decide how to nurture them, or whether it is better to sideline them. As the winner of a clutch of Maverick of the Year awards, I tend to prefer embracing those who zig when everybody else zags.

O The child-like ones. Learn how to appreciate their values of curiosity, excitement, faith and trust. Walt Disney once said, 'That's the real trouble with the world. Too many people grow up.'

O The in-laws. Learn how to reformat the business family following acquisitions and mergers.

O Tribes and clans. Understand the power of company, and industry-wide, togetherness.

This variety is what adds to the potential power of any group of people. Rather than trying to turn everyone into the same automaton, recognising difference allows you to marshal your forces, even if sometimes it feels as if you are herding cars (and anyone who has had the pleasure of rounding up small children, cat owner or not, will know that feeling far too well). Equally, it can create an environment where the potential for conflict is never far away.

## A TIME OF CONFLICT

In his talks, the psychologist Oliver James refers to an analysis of the mental state of senior managers which revealed that, in three out of eleven specific areas, those managers had more personality disorders than psychiatric patients and prisoners in Broadmoor. It made me wonder whether part of being successful at work requires you to be slightly unbalanced, which may impact adversely on the likelihood of a balanced, stable home life.

Oliver James uses that example to pose the question: should we create a society where we don't push people to be in that space? For example, we are living in an era of unprecedented affluence, regardless of where we are on the scale, but personal relationships are often dysfunctional. Our mindset is this: if I move to London I will get a better job. If I get a better job I will get more successful. If I get a different job I will be more successful. I am stuck in a rut so I will change something. Inevitably, we use the same thinking when it comes to relationships, which is why divorce rates have gone up through the roof: I am unhappy therefore I will change it, rather than work at it.

In the same way, many people aspire to a better car. Well, a car is a car is a car. It gets you from A to B unless it is completely unreliable, but one car is largely the same as another – except that it is an indicator and a perception of how we are seen.

Society has become about *having* rather than *being*. Having something rather than being happy; a 'me, me, me' culture. There is a point of view that, these days, equal opportunity has not led to us become more caring. In many cases women have adopted the worst aspects of male selfishness. This narcissism can be based on a worthless feeling: if you are badly treated as a child, you become insecure; therefore you become narcissistic to prove your self-worth. I know that many will find this view controversial, but it is certainly worthy of debate.

According to Oliver James, if we want our children to function, rewards and punishments need to be present, but the punishment element is often forgotten. As children get older and we push them at school, to do their homework, go for extra tutoring, they don't think, 'Ah, you're doing that for my good', they just think you're shouting at them again. We don't teach them that it's a natural part of life to have to overcome difficulties.

This is exacerbated by the D-word: disruption. In many, if not most, industries change (good and healthy in the long term) is having a short-term negative impact. A rapid rate of change, a sense of uncertainty and insecurity, leads to a feeling of inadequacy, and in turn to a defensiveness that infects business and personal relationships. It can create a feeling of alienation in the home, and affect our personal sense of self-worth. Whether at home or at work, someone who feels under threat or under-valued is going to get angry. And anger fuels conflict.

Sometimes that anger and conflict is self-induced, the result of a self-destructive streak. I was intrigued by the example of Sam Allardyce, who had spent 25 years as a football manager working towards his goal, his dream job: to be the manager of the England football team. He achieved it in July 2016. A mere 67 days later he was out of a job, following allegations of malpractice. He blew it, his life's objective, in two months. Was it through bravado, or idiocy?

Allardyce was angry. He said 'entrapment has won the day'. Well, you never *have* to be entrapped. When you get caught by a speed camera, it is not the police's fault. Even if he had shown an error of judgement, his integrity was flawed. As Warren Buffett put it, 'If you lose money for the firm I will be understanding. If you lose my reputation I will be ruthless.'

Right at the point of conflict, at the very time where every-one is feeling stressed out, is the best moment to seek a different way. Psychologist Brenda Shoshanna has said that all the con-flict we experience is the result of a conflict within ourselves. So it's within our gift to deal with it in a different, better way.

Instead of getting angry, think about an alternative path. *Negotiation* should be the new norm, learning how to *com-promise*. The more 'powerful' you are within an organisation, the more humble you should be prepared to be, and the more willing to make the first conciliatory gesture. If you have the power, you can afford to be generous with it.

# COPING WITH STRESS AND CONFLICT

It's official. Conflict is bad for you. Constant arguing leads to a risk of an early death. A Danish research team under Dr Rikke Lund at the University of Copenhagen found that frequent arguments with your wife, husband, partner, friends or family, and dealing with their worries and demands, significantly increases the mortality rate in middle age, especially among men.

When I was running the 40 marathons in the summer of 2016, many people told me that running was their way of releasing stress, coping with conflict, shaking things up: 'When I am stressed, stuck in a rut, I go for a run. It clears my mind.' Oddly this doesn't work for me, but it's good to find your own way to cut through that stress cycle, the spiral of angst, self-pity and self-centred resentment that can so often drag you down.

I have personally tried to learn how to convert negative emotions into positive solutions, not least when I am building up to an argument. My relationship with my wife now is different to all my relationships with my previous wives. In the past, my reaction to an argument would have been, 'Well, **** that, then.' Now, when we argue, I say,

*OK, one of us has gone into a strop. Let's fast-forward, because I know for sure that this relationship is not ending. Are we clear? 'Yes.' So at some point between now and ten years from now we are going to have to get over this; otherwise we are going to have a really awful life together. So can we fast-forward to that point, and do that now and be happy and smiley, agree to disagree or talk about it more rationally?*

We learn from arguments with loved ones that they are rarely a binary 'yes' or 'no'.

You build up to an argument – zippp… – and that's exactly the moment you should be talking. So again: 'Can we simply fast-forward to the point where we are making up?' Which actually makes my wife laugh and helps break down the tension of the moment. Taking the conflict out of the situation enables you to see the disagreement in simpler terms.

At this stage in business, you'd probably say, 'Could we agree this, and then work from there towards a final agreement,' which usually works. It's called compromise.

In our business lives we are constantly making compromises, finding a solution that has benefits for both sides (even if we are in fact trying to find a solution that has more tangible benefits for us). It's par for the course in a working day. And yet at home we would rather sit there in a strop, frustrated and unhappy, than do what we do every day in business: find the middle road to be able to make progress.

## COMPROMISE REQUIRES TIME

A lot of business advice suggests that compromise is a sign of weakness, that the compromise solution is the worst of all possible options. I would suggest that compromise – as long as you share the same goals – is, in fact, a strength. In the past, I was also less than keen on the word 'compromise', but I now recognise its value, provided, of course, that you don't compromise your vision or your values at the same time.

This shift in perception is something you have to work at. It's not a one-off. In the dressing room at Twickenham rugby stadium, one of the phrases on the wall reminds the England players that winning is only about getting up one more time when you fall down.

When I brought in Jagdish, the yogi, to work with my management team, I still had to bring him back every year. Otherwise we all started slipping back into old patterns of behaviour. Others would say they didn't need another session; that they had learnt what he had to teach them. But changing your way of operating and thinking is not a one-off exam with a diploma you can display on the wall. It is a continuous process, because people are essentially lazy. You need to invest time.

The Wisdom 2.0 conference is a gathering of business leaders, life coaches, tech entrepreneurs and neuroscientists, with a mission to 'foster wisdom and wellness in the technology industry'. 'Just a few years ago,' the organisers say, 'you would never have imagined the executives of leading technology firms joining together with yoga teachers, meditation instructors, and people who talk about chi in everyday conversation to plan for business of the future.' *Wired* magazine described the summit as 'where the technology and contemplative communities hash out the best ways to incorporate these [technological] tools into our lives – and keep them from taking over'.

Wisdom 2.0's founder, Soren Gordhamer, called it one of the great challenges of our age: 'to not only live connected to one another through technology, but to do so in ways that are beneficial to our own well-being, effective in our work, and useful to the world'. One of the messages of this book is that technology is something that will benefit us all in achieving work/life integration: being open to working with a yogi while exploring the potential of technology is the kind of combination that is going to be increasingly the norm.

Mike Broderick, the CEO of Turning Technologies, which produces interactive response technology, has written about using that technology to resolve conflict at work:

*In any organization involving a group, conflict is virtually inevitable. People have different values, ideas, style and personalities, and occasionally they will clash. For many managers, handling workplace conflicts is one of the most stressful aspects of the job.*

*However, conflict isn't necessarily a negative. When employees are passionate about their work and truly care about delivering the best service to customers, sometimes conflicts can arise, and the process of resolving them can provide everyone involved with new insights that can shape future behaviour. Some conflicts are corrosive to staff morale. But what about conflicts that involve a clash between business philosophies or that arise because of an operational change that affects employees? Differing opinions on how the company will move forward are normal when a major change is contemplated, and effective leaders can influence employee perceptions while aligning efforts with organizational goals.*

Broderick states that polling software allows company leaders to ask questions or lead discussions by embedding questions into presentations and enabling individuals to respond anonymously via a clicker or smartphone. This promotes open discussion, gives every employee a voice, lets everyone know where the group stands, and indicates when a consensus has been reached. It's an example of how technology offers a way of applying a different approach to conflict.

## TAKING TIME

In the movie *In Time*, Justin Timberlake plays Ohio factory worker Will Salas; the film is set in 2169. By that time people have been genetically engineered to enjoy perfect health and appearance. The world's population is getting too big, so there has to be a way of culling people. On their 25th birthday, each individual's time starts running out and a digital clock imprinted on their forearm begins counting down the time they have left. This depends on the time capsule you exist in; for Will Salas in Ohio, time is short. In wealthy, time-rich areas, people have more time than they can use, and time is a worthless thing.

Even if you are in a time-poor zone, you can work to earn time credits, or you can exchange time with another person who has more time than you. Money doesn't exist. Money has been replaced by time. So you can charge up your digital clock – or someone can mug you and steal your time.

At one point in the film, Salas's mother has to pay off a loan, payable in time, which leaves her short of the time she needs to get home by bus. Salas has got some spare time because he has worked extra hours. His mother urges him to find her, and meanwhile starts running down the road because, if she doesn't get to him, she will die. They nearly find each other, but they are seconds too late. All they needed was more time. She would have given anything, all that she owned, for another ten seconds, because those ten seconds were so valuable.

Time and money are currencies. We focus on spending time to get money only to get to a point in our lives where we realise that we are spending money to get more time. When you are young, time is irrelevant. All you want to do is earn money. You squander time. Then, at a certain point, when you realise that you are getting older, you spend money to get time back, perhaps on better doctors, on cosmetic surgery.

Time is constantly being spent: you spend it or it gets spent. And you can't genuinely *save* time, even with labour-saving devices. So, if we invest time by investing respect, commitment, love in other people, we will see a much better, more productive return on that investment.

## THE POWER OF POSITIVITY, THE DOWNWARD DRAG OF NEGATIVITY

When I am on a roll, feeling upbeat and positive, I find it difficult to cope with negative people. It is like being in a soundproof box, with all my positivity disappearing into a black hole. I enjoy situations where something I say or suggest triggers a discussion and the ideas flow. My ideas rebound, like a reflective sound. I am sure that is true of all of us.

That's the opposite of the feeling you get when, say, a plumber comes round and the first thing he does is suck his breath in, shake his head and say, 'Oh, no, no, no...' I was once at a comedy show where the stand-up said, 'Imagine if the fire brigade were like plumbers, turned up, took one look at your fire and shook their heads: "Oh, no, I'm going to need a hose for that, I haven't got one." ' The reality, of course, is that the emergency services, like the military, turn up at a situation with a massively positive attitude, a fix-it mentality, a total non-acceptance of failure. Apologies to all plumbers out there for the comedic stereotyping – I am indebted to a number of great plumbers – and the stakes involved are different between a plumber and a firefighter, but you get my point.

I was having a huge amount of building work done at

home. Steve, the main builder, was absolutely brilliant, even when disaster loomed: we had a huge leak and were panicking. Steve came in, calmly assessed the situation and told us, 'It's OK. I'll bring in this guy to sort that, we'll cover everything up so the furniture is dustproofed, paint the ceiling and the walls back up. It will be done by Thursday and you won't even know we've been here.' That's the ability to own a situation and also to know who to bring in to solve a problem. We may not have the knowledge to solve a problem ourselves, but if we know who we can ask to help us, where the technical answers can be found, that is true delegation: respecting the abilities of others to help us in a crisis.

This allows us to unblock the logjam. So often conflict, outward or inner, comes from some hidden blockage we choose not to identify or confront. If we imagine ourselves constantly coming back to the same thing – I *must* make that phone call, I must make it – it helps to identify what's preventing us from doing it, to find out what is the mental block.

A handy technique is to ask *why*. Why are you afraid to make that call? Well, because they might turn me down… Why are you worried that they might turn you down? Well, because… etc., etc. – until you run out of reasons.

Asking and answering those whys often gives you a starting point for unblocking the issue. You'll probably find that the situation is not as bad as you originally thought, and that you'll be able to bust the block and move on.

## LETTING GO, LEAVING ROOM FOR LOVE

To end this section on love, I want to share with you

something my brother wrote for me when my father died. I disliked my father for the many bad things he did in his life and the impact that had on my family. I didn't go to his funeral and I didn't care about his passing. This was my brother's attempt to try and put his life into perspective and to search out forgiveness. This does not apply only to family, or to people that have died, but to business and relationships up and down the scale.

*Life has taught me that:*

*None of us undergo an apprenticeship for living a good life and, at some stage, we all make poor life decisions and do bad things.*

*While the conditions of our life commonly shape our choices, ultimately it's our decisions that determine our destiny.*

*No matter what each day brings or how bad life appears at dusk, the dawn brings new opportunities. Sometimes, only sometimes, happenstance gives us a second chance to steer destiny back on track.*

*We become who we are, from our very beginning, but even more so towards the end. As we grow, we learn that what is right is far more transparent than knowing what is true.*

*Regardless of our relationship with our parents, progressively, we will miss them deeply when they are no longer in our life.*

*In their own way and in the context of the circumstances at the time, both my parents tried to protect me from harm and allowed me to feel loved.*

*While spoken words can burn deep and leave scars never to be erased, our real agony stems from the words unsaid to those we have lost. While people will forget exactly what was said and exactly what was done, they will never forget how they were made to feel.*

*Courage, truth, loyalty, humility and ingenuous compassion are uncommon human virtues.*

*I still have a lot to learn, but, given the opportunity to revisit the beings I have harmed, I hope for the chance to put right my wrongs.*

Wise words indeed.

# QR: AUGMENTED DISCOVERY

Click on the QR code at the end of this chapter. You'll instantly download clips of me telling you more about each of these key points:

- Businesses are like families. In fact, they are like families who spend more time together, and under more pressure, than those at home.

- Anyone knows that family arguments can rarely be resolved by a simple 'yes' or 'no' – otherwise it turns into a parental powerplay and/or a slanging match.

- Being big enough to take the first step towards compromise will usually pay huge dividends; conciliation also reflects well on you. Finding a middle road is not a climb-down: it's just pragmatism.

- Conflict is not necessarily a bad thing per se: it may be proof of a real passion and belief, and that someone is prepared to stand up for those beliefs. Find out why.

- Invest time as wisely as you would ideally like to with

your own money. Invest it in respect, commitment and love, and see the super-positive returns that can accrue.

*'I realised that I love my life. I really do. I've got the greatest family in the world, and I've got my work. And that's pretty much all I do. I get to do that. I'm very lucky.'*

Steve Jobs

# Part III

# WORK

# Chapter 7

MT

WORK SMART, TAKE HEART

# WORK SMART, TAKE HEART

## Multiplying your effectiveness

*'There's no such thing as work/life balance. There are work/life choices, and you make them, and there are consequences.'*

General Electric CEO Jack Welch

Work is not what we used to think it was. Those four simple, sometimes terrifying, letters mask a myriad of meanings, memories and memes.

The wall that once existed between work and family has been permanently breached. The nuclear family beloved of Ladybird books is no more – it is a throwback to a distant, golden-tinged, rose-tinted age (which quite probably never actually existed) of 2.4 children and a father coming home from a day at the office or the factory to find his wife and kids sitting round the dinner table with glowing happy faces.

Work was a separate entity, something that happened outside the home, which could be hung on a peg and forgotten about as easily as father's trilby, and was purely an activity to enable the nuclear family to be kept, fed, watered and contented. The truth is of course that work and life are now completely unrecognisable from that nostalgic image. The frontiers are blurred, fragmented and increasingly redundant. Twenty-five years on from the emergence of the internet, the omnipresence of the web in our lives has changed everything.

Over the past few decades there has been much written about the so-called work/life balance. The phrase seems to have originally been coined sometime in the 1970s, although it is difficult to pin down a precise first usage. It then gained a foothold during the 1980s as a fairly broad term that suggested that highly driven, or overworked, staff never had enough hours in the day to spend quality time with their family.

As the divorce rate rose and single-parent families became increasingly common, while more women went to work to boost the family income, the sense of work/life developed a more negative connotation, upping the guilt factor of parents leaving their children behind to be looked after by relatives, nannies or childminders, or plonking them in after-school clubs waiting for a commuting mum or dad to come and collect them.

What lay at the heart of the phrase was that work and life were somehow different: discrete activities that needed a separate focus and attention. You could work, or you could have a life, but you could not do both at the same time.

I'd suggest another way of looking at this:

*Work/life is not a divide. It should be a multiple.*

If there is any kind of a balance involved, it is about making choices – the right choices for you.

That's why I believe that talking about balance between work and life is completely the wrong focus. As I have already suggested, you simply cannot be outstanding in two activities and have balance between them, that idea that you can't be both a world champion marathon runner and a world champion weightlifter. But if you choose a different focus, you could be a world-class decathlete.

It is, of course, easy to write about this, but far, far harder to do it. For many people this is a pipe dream, an aspiration. For anyone who does still have a 9-to-5 job – and more importantly a 9-to-5 responsibility – it may seem that there is no need for work/life integration. One could say that a bus driver, for example, works a shift and at the end goes home with no job 'liabilities'. But I disagree. He or she could have had a very stressful day, take that stress back home and in doing so could drive a rift through the home relationship. To avoid this, the same principles of inclusion of a partner or spouse at home in the issues of the day should apply.

## WORKING TO LIVE, OR LIVING TO WORK

The computing power contained inside any smartphone is immense compared to even five years ago. It is easy, convenient, tempting to work everywhere: the home, the park, the coffee shop or the bedroom can become a convenient potential workspace – one that may happen to contain your family members rather than your work colleagues.

The received opinion is that this is a negative. When the Blackberry was being dubbed the 'Crackberry', the message was that using a phone to check emails and to keep on top of work was nothing less than an addiction. That's behind the rise in a series of contemporary aphorisms like 'Life is what happens to you when you're looking at your smartphone' or 'We live in an era of smart phones and stupid people'.

All those pithy sayings have a certain element of truth at

their heart, but they are dressed up in an attitude of negativity towards technology, which – as someone who has worked in the technology sector for decades, and who sees the many positive benefits it can bring – I find a little depressing.

I want to make the distinction between balance and integration. Balance would be working really hard for months, then taking a vacation and declaring, 'You know what? I am on holiday. I have taken this week off. And that means "off". It's been in the diary for aeons, so no, I am not taking that call or answering that mail. I am off-air and off-line. End of.'

Integration is thinking, 'I am having a great holiday, I am enjoying spending time with the family, relaxing, recharging and refreshing myself. So I can easily fit into the structure of our day a small window that doesn't interfere with my family time or my own "me" time to catch up on some emails and see if anything is genuinely pressing from a work point of view or even just keeping the volume down for when I get back home.'

## WE ARE WORKING TOO HARD

Many of us are working too hard, putting in long hours, continuing to work outside the office. Some say this is because of bullying bosses; others, that we are driven by economic or cultural forces or by ambition or pride.

Whatever the reason, research shows we are working harder and the reality is that working too hard doesn't work. It leads to health problems including lack of sleep, diabetes or heart disease. And in turn that it is not good for a company's bottom line, with increased levels of absenteeism, high staff turnover, less effective working, more mistakes.

In the UK in 2015–16, the Health and Safety Executive calculated that there were 488,000 – getting on for half a million

– cases of work-related stress, depression or anxiety: in the same year, 11.7 million days were directly lost as a result of all of those problems (some might say excuses). Of the days lost to ill-health, 45 per cent were due to stress.

According to Jacquelyn Smith in the *Independent*,

*Everybody's working for the weekend, but how you spend those two days may say something about how successful you are. What you get up to doesn't really matter, per se. If you prefer lounging around the house to spontaneous adventures, that's great. You probably need that time to wind down. When it comes to weekends, the main thing that separates successful people from unsuccessful people is mindfulness.*

Here's Jenny Coad of the *Spectator*, writing in early 2017:

*On a Friday evening in May 2018 I am going to see the Broadway show* Hamilton. *We had to book the tickets two weeks ago. Fair enough, you might say – some theatre tickets sell out long before rehearsals have begun. Nonetheless, it seems a madly long way off and what if I forget about it between now and then? This week I've tried to pencil in the cinema with a group of friends – no one was free until April – and Saturday supper with a couple: they couldn't do until July.*

This is far from unusual. My diary tends to be filled weeks in advance and there is little room for unexpected pleasures without a shamefaced untangling of best-laid plans. Most of us are masters at unpicking things that sounded like a nice idea at the time. The builder is in. The children are poorly. I'm stuck at work. All of which makes me wonder if we are over-organising our lives for no good reason at all. Being busy for the sake of it. Whatever happened to spontaneity? Even free time has become a thing we cling to, written in our diaries in bold, desperate caps: **KEEP FREE.**

On 1 January 2017, France's 'right to disconnect' law came into effect. The law obliges organisations with over 50 employees to initiate 'switching off' negotiations with their workforces. The goal of the negotiations is for everyone to agree on employees' rights to ignore work-related requests outside the boundaries of regular work hours. If employer and employees cannot come to a satisfactory compromise, the organisation must publish a charter that explicitly defines employee rights with respect to out-of-hours communication.

Surprisingly, some employers are embracing it more than their employees. 'There's a real expectation that companies will seize on the "right to disconnect" as a protective measure,' French workplace expert and ARISTAT director Xavier Zunigo said when the law was launched. 'At the same time, workers don't want to lose the autonomy and flexibility that digital devices give them.'

## THE BEAUTY OF LATERAL THINKING

In the nineteenth century, when organised labour first compelled factory owners to limit work hours per day to ten and then eight, management was surprised to discover that output actually increased and that expensive accidents and mistakes decreased. The same thinking applies just as well to today's knowledge workers. It's a lesson we need to relearn.

So working smarter, not harder, is how we need to think. There is a famous example used in management training sessions of a Pittsburgh-based steel company in the 1890s. They had stockpiled thousands of tons of pig-iron and now needed it urgently loaded onto train carriages. The boss told his senior management that they needed to shift more goods: so off went one manager who told the labourers to essentially 'work harder'. He upped the rate of loading, but very few people could handle the pitiless workload. A British engineer visiting the company noticed that the workers were all young and vigorous. 'Where are all your old workers?' he asked. His guide offered him a cigar, and invited him to visit the cemetery.

The converse of that insistence on simply working harder – with all its detrimental effects – is the 'Pomodoro Technique', developed by Francesco Cirillo, an Italian business studies student. A century on from the pig-iron approach, in the 1980s and 1990s he suggested breaking down work into intervals of approximately 25 minutes, with short breaks in between: his theory was that productivity would be vastly increased (he named the technique after his kitchen timer, which was shaped like a tomato – 'pomodoro' in Italian).

That's the 'work smarter' approach. The creative solution. Creative is not saying you are working harder and faster for ten hours, it's about, perhaps, staging it. This kind of creativity is in danger of disappearing. When we are kids we are super-creative and then we unlearn it all. Why are we doing that?

We are surrounded, especially in a business environment, by messages that encourage conformity: labels, uniforms, the fixed desks in an open-plan office, identical screens – everyone looks exactly the same. Schools are obsessed with planification and control, and teachers have hardly any freedom to operate outside the constraints of an imposed curriculum.

The environmentalist and social advocate George Monbiot has written that, in an age of robots, schools are teaching children to be redundant. He says that in the future, to create a job for yourself, you will need be as

*unlike a machine as possible: creative, critical and socially skilled. So why are children being taught to be like machines?*

*Children learn best when teaching aligns with their natural exuberance, energy and curiosity.*

He quotes as an example the first multiracial school in South Africa, Woodmead, where students were involved in creating the curriculum, following their natural interests. The school has produced many of South Africa's current leaders, across all aspects of society. In Monbiot's words, 'Let's have some social engineering. Let's engineer out children out of the factory and into the real world.'

## COMING OUT OF THE PIGEONHOLE

In the film *Divergent*, the premise is that when children reach a certain age, they are labelled. You are either a 'fighter' or a 'worker' or an 'intelligent', but you can't be all of them. You are not allowed to have traits of everything, because then you are dangerous and unpredictable. You have to be pigeonholed into one of these categories and then everyone knows how to manage you.

Company management always tells staff, 'We want you to be innovative, we need innovation, creativity', and yet they don't drive it. Much of that comes from the fear of looking stupid. A colleague once passed on to me the thought that 'if your first idea on the new product isn't stupid, then it's not worth being a first idea because somebody has probably already done it'.

Forget the fear of looking stupid. There is one fear that says, 'Do you actually think that you are not creative? If I try to be creative and we establish that I'm not, that makes me a failure from the beginning.' That creates a self-definition which virtually excludes the possibility of being creative in the first place.

Here technology plays its part. David Hockney is one of the greatest, if not *the* greatest, living British artist. He has always been at the cutting edge of technology, whether collaging Polaroids, being a pioneer of the early adoption of the iPad in art, drawing straight onto screens, and then returning to painting more traditional portraits, comfortable with any medium, any technology, not blinkered but not discarding old-style techniques. Thinking about cutting edges reminds me of a phrase that was current in the 1980s, when home computers were starting to emerge as affordable purchases: 'When you are working on the cutting edge of technology, the main thing is to stay behind the blade.'

*'Everything worth fighting for unbalances your life.'*
Alain de Botton

## WORKING OUR BRAIN MUSCLES

If we allow technology to make us lazy, then we will become lazy. I know that in the age before mobiles I could recall every single telephone number of the important people in my life, reel them off instantly. I could do the same with the registration plates of every car I had ever owned. Now, like everyone else, I can barely remember my wife's number – because it's plugged into the contacts on my phone. It's in the machine, always there.

So I am no longer massaging that particular slice of brain muscle. On the other hand (or lobe, perhaps), I am freeing up memory space for more useful items. It depends what you replace that memory space with. Do we work hard to save time, use technology to save time, to then just waste it? Or do we do something productive with it? We need to be more conscious of our choices, in how we deploy that time.

One thing I consciously try to do is remember people's names. That is a valuable use of brain space. We are living in an age when individual identity is harder to sustain – just enter the things you believe make you unique on Google, and you'll find rafts of people who fit the same profile. In China you could be one in a million, but there will still be 1,378 other people exactly like you.

So when I meet anyone new, and particularly a group of people all at the same time in a large meeting or a work event, I often check with them how their names are spelt, partly because people are often quite sensitive and protective of their names, but also because checking the spelling imprints it in my mind. 'Is that Theresa with an h? Philip with one or two ls?' I can store that trigger in the part of my brain where those phone numbers used to sit, and retrieve it later on in the evening, or in a month's or a year's time.

For Timo Kiander, author of *Work Smarter Not Harder*, the core building blocks of an active mind are a combination of:

*Proper mindset + physical activity + optimum nutrition + enough sleep.*

From his list of core requirements, I would highlight:

O  A powerful start to the day

O  Never starting your day unplanned

O  Thinking ahead about meetings

O  Delegating the right way

O  Taking care of the 'frogs' (those overwhelming problem items on your daily list) right away.

All of this contributes to the flexibility that is vital for success in life and work. Mark Batey, a senior lecturer in organisational psychology at Alliance Manchester Business School, has written:

*This is the human era of the workplace. The best places to work are those in which people can flourish and be their best selves – instead of pretending to be someone else five days a week. The perfect workplace also gives people flexibility and autonomy as to where and how they work, built on a culture of growth and trust.*

We should also be mindful of the multiplication that is generated by diversity. Linda Jackson, writing in the *Guardian* about the launch in May 2017 of a new British Standard recognising the fact that people are a company's most valuable assets, said, 'Genuine diversity and inclusion across British organisations still has some way to go.'

In the same spirit of multiplication, organisations can play an active role in encouraging their staff to take a broader view of the business environment. For example, the company Pivotal Network runs regular 'lunch and learn' sessions aimed at introducing topics from technology to business education, increasing employees' broader knowledge and encouraging better communication and collaboration.

A cautionary note: I read that some research conducted at Stanford University revealed that 'multi-tasking is less productive than doing a single thing at a time, that people who are regularly bombarded with several streams of electronic information cannot pay attention, recall information, or switch from one job to another as well as those who complete one task at a time.' I'm not sure I agree, and I'm sure my children definitely would not agree. My opinion is that future generations will be far better at multi-tasking than any previous ones.

# THINKING SMARTER

A couple of years ago, the organisers of an event in Monaco for the data centre industry asked me to create a publicity video to encourage people to attend. They wanted delegates who had attended the event the year before to take a video of themselves explaining why the event was important to attend. On the spur of the moment, walking down a London street, I simply shot a selfie video, complete with traffic noise and people walking past looking at me strangely... The organisers ran a competition for the best video based on the most views, and I won it outright. They told me that virtually no one voted for any other entry, because my video was alive, vibrant, real.

The next year they asked me whether I could do something even more out there to promote their event. The words of the message were straightforward and frankly dull: 'If you want to know everything there is to know about data centres in Africa, the risks, the opportunities, the chance to make a fortune, come to Invest in Data Center Africa in Monaco 2016.' This time I wanted to do something outlandish and found an app which gave me the face of The Joker from the *Batman* movie for the video. Again I told people why they should attend the event, but my face looked as scary as The Joker's, and I imitated his voice. I was trying to shock them. When I sent the results over, the organisers weren't sure, they said it was too shocking. 'I know you want it to be creative, but that's just too creative for us.' But then they watched it again and relented.

This was not about the technology itself, but about using technology as a tool. Taking the footage and enhancing it was not the key: it was the idea in the first place. That was an example of thinking smarter.

# WORKING WITH FOCUS – OVERCOMING PROCRASTINATION

We resolve to tackle a task and then find lots of reasons why we should defer it, prioritising those items we can easily tick off, but pushing the large, complex items further and further away, so those problems seem more daunting in our mind. Whether they are in reality or not, they eventually become too big to deal with. Our brains are programmed to procrastinate; we struggle with tasks which only promise a future, sometimes distant, upside in return for efforts we have to take now: it's a case of short-term gain vs long-term promise.

When I left TelecityGroup I was in the fortunate position of being able to forsake a safe full-time role with a steady monthly salary to spend three years building a portfolio of investments and non-executive roles. I received very little income over that period, but my hope and expectation was that after three years my investment in time and effort would be returned through successful exits of those investments on a regular basis. After being used to having a salary, though, making that mental leap was still quite difficult.

It is easier for our brains to process concrete tasks than abstract potential. Our brain strives hard to shape the abstract into the concrete, to clean up the stuff it can't process. Short-term effort always dominates long-term upside. Behavioural scientists call this 'present bias'.

We are averse to the proper evaluation of the status quo; we prefer to weigh up the pros and cons of something else rather than those of the here and now. When people are asked in a referendum to vote for something different or the same, they may often choose change because it is much harder to evaluate the state of play today. By evaluating the effects of 'no action', we can clarify the benefits of action. If you force yourself to think about the downside of putting something off, then you quickly realise the value of action now.

Equally you can break down the difficult step into smaller steps. When I was running the 40 marathons, by the third day, thinking of the next 37 to come was beyond my ability to comprehend. There was no way I believed I could do it. So I had to think of not just the next marathon, but one more step, the next of the 42,000 steps coming up. So, instead of wanting to learn French but thinking, 'I'll never be able to do that, with everything else that's going on in my life', you could start by sending an email to someone for advice on whether it would be better to use Rosetta Stone or Babel; a small step, taking you that little bit further along the way. The achievement of small goals is what keeps you motivated.

And you should reward yourself for each step or series of steps – a guilty pleasure, like a treat, a glass of champagne. That dilutes the brain's perception of long-term effort/reward, and provides a splash of instant gratification, a reward at that point for the effort put in.

# QR: AUGMENTED DISCOVERY

Click on the QR code at the end of this chapter. You'll instantly download clips of me telling you more about each of these key points.

- The boundaries that existed clearly between work and home have been obliterated once and for all. That era of a 9-to-5 day spent 'at work' seems now so archaic as to date from a cheery illustration in a Ladybird book.

■ The concepts of 'family' and 'home' have undergone such radical change in recent years that both the language we use and its application to the way we work demand a complete mental reboot. The clichéd phrase 'work/life balance', suggesting two separate unconnected activities, is now redundant.

■ We should be talking about the integration of work and life, where what we do at any moment in the day exists within all our other activities. This does not mean that our ability to work or to live is threatened or limited by either. In fact, it is liberating.

■ We need to free up our minds by taking off the blinkers of procrastination, and by not worrying about looking stupid – and not getting pigeonholed.

■ By channelling all of the possibilities offered by the chance to work when, where and how we want we can actually greatly increase our effectiveness in every sphere of our lives: a work/life multiple rather than a divide.

> '*We tend to forget that happiness doesn't come as a result of getting something we don't have, but rather of recognising and appreciating what we do have.*'
>
> Friedrich Koenig

MT

WORK SMART, TAKE HEART

# Chapter 8

MT

WORK IS RELATIVE

# WORK IS RELATIVE

## Where work and family are closely intertwined

*'Don't let personal differences or egos cloud
your judgement – the business is more important
than any individual family member.'*

Jonathan Warburton, Warburtons Bakeries

I was in Shanghai, spending some time understanding the cultures and methodologies of doing business in China, when I came across an example that has stuck with me: Confucius's concept of living in harmony was adopted by the French company Carrefour, the retailer that was at the frontline of the hypermarket revolution in the 1960s and 1970s.

The name of Carrefour in Chinese is made up of three Chinese characters: Jia (family), Le (joy), and Fu (happiness). The message is that the representation of a happy family is the key to success – and harmony is the base of Confucian philosophy. Does that mean balance, or integration?

If the overlap between life and work, between family and business, is now virtually complete, can we learn anything from family businesses? They might seem in some ways like a rather outdated concept, but consider these facts:

O In the US, family businesses represent 57 per cent of national GDP, create 80 per cent of new jobs and make up one third of the Fortune 500.

O In the UK, 60 per cent of SMEs are family run. The family running its own business is a crucial part of the economy...

O ... and that is despite the fact that only 30 per cent of family businesses transfer successfully to the second generation (and only 3 per cent to the fourth generation).

## THE PROS AND CONS OF KEEPING IT IN THE FAMILY

Some family companies are happy to remain small – what in America are affectionately called 'mom and pop' stores. Here the focus is on resilience and robustness sometimes more than on performance. But equally other family businesses have grown into hugely powerful multinationals: Walmart, Samsung, Tata, Porsche, Mittal and Ford. There are no hard and fast rules.

The combination of family and business can clearly be a good thing. There might be different expectations: the possibility that the glue of family relationships – and being used to coping with the endless tricky diplomacy of family politics – will help the company to survive difficult times; an implicit sense of trust that is literally innate; a longer-term viewpoint that contrasts positively with short-term thinking.

Xenios Thrasyvoulou, the founder of People Per Hour, one

of the companies I'm involved in, wrote about one positive aspect of family and business in the *Huffington Post*. In 2013 he observed:

*One in five small business owners has turned to the bank of 'friends and family' for start-up capital, and almost three-quarters launched their new business ventures with working capital of £2,000 or less. Of the 5,000 small business owners polled, 76 per cent said they had to use their own personal savings as working capital, while 13 per cent said that redundancy money provided their start-up funds. Only 3 per cent of small business owners polled said they were able to secure a bank loan to get their business off the ground; this highlighted the banks' reluctance to lend to riskier start-ups. As a result, business owners have been forced to look elsewhere for funding to get their ventures off the ground.*

The flip side of involving the family in business is that emotions, feuds and unspoken anger, left unattended because of embarrassment or a misplaced loyalty, can fester and implode. In a family business it can be difficult to achieve the right level of separation, the independence to make decisions. Family 'love' gets in the way.

In non-family businesses, dissatisfaction between a board and a CEO, between a boss and a member of staff or between colleagues, is usually and ultimately resolved by one party moving on, voluntarily or with a helping hand. And life returns to some form of normal, with the conflict, at least temporarily, suppressed.

You can't resign from a family in quite the same way. Firing a family member brings a whole raft of ramifications and repercussions with it. Yet nepotism is not always the answer either.

# BUCKING THE MACHO CULTURE

Even though testosterone-fuelled machismo is on the wane, it still has its adherents. The film *The Wolf of Wall Street*, even in the supposedly enlightened 2010s, still became a cult movie for certain traders who had never quite got over their nostalgic view of the original 1980s Wall Street ball-busting mentality.

And there are still far too many examples of dictatorial, 'father figure' bosses, who believe they are always right, who cannot understand why anyone else would disagree with them, and who, when things don't go to their plan, lurch into apoplectic spleen, rancour and threats; hardly conducive to inspiring loyalty from those working for them. All they inspire is reciprocal anger, wasted time and resigned bemusement or fear, none of which is productive.

Imagine all that within the powder keg of a family business. Imagine that mindset as it returns from the office to the family home: that sense of the big businessman wondering just why his kids don't immediately do what he asks them to. For him, teenage attitude is akin to insubordination.

My wife Shalina comes from an Indian family. India has a long tradition of family businesses. I recently came across a piece of research by John L. Ward, who is a professor at the Kellogg School of Management in Chicago. He believes that, in particular, Indian business groups are more likely to split up because they often fail to involve daughters in the family business.

He says, 'A family that only has brothers at the helm is the most unstable form of business enterprise. Brothers often end up with ego issues. If you involve daughters and other female members of the family then the bond is stronger.'

However, for long-standing cultural reasons, Indian family

businesses rarely allow girls into management. The boys' egos are unrestrained; they end up rutting like stags. Daughters involved in the business will often create a better bond between all the family members.

As the report pointed out, 'This stands to reason. It is criminal not to deploy 50 per cent of the business talent.' Surely a workforce that reflects the make-up of society is going to be far more durable?

Another company sent its (exclusively male) management team and their spouses to a retreat. While the management team was in its offsite meeting, the wives had their own session within the schedule where it was explained to them exactly what their husbands could and should do to get a promotion. The company believed that having the spouses convince their husbands to change their attitudes and achieve success worked better than having the men go head to head in the existing hierarchy. Now that's an example of a different concept of family–business integration, albeit one that assumes a rather traditional domestic set-up.

A business that possesses the richness of diversity and the odd black sheep – just like a family does – is more likely to succeed than one composed of clones of the business leader. Everyone within a family can be an entrepreneur.

Even in an era of globalisation, cultural differences persist. I went to a *Spectator* magazine talk, the theme of which was 'Will Britain ever have a Facebook?' The subtext was that, in the USA, if you fail you are applauded. You obviously can't keep failing at the same thing, but if you fail in one venture people assume that you have learnt from your experience and that repeating the mistake is something they will not have to worry about in their risk profile of you. You have done it and you won't do it again. By contrast, in the UK, if you have one or two failures you are toast.

In certain countries – in parts of Africa, on the Indian subcontinent – a widow or a divorced woman is stigmatised, because, completely unfairly, her life is considered a failure. Although all sorts of circumstances might have conspired against her, including illness or war, it is unusual for such women to be respected as they should be: as more resilient, more aware, more knowledgeable because of having lived through that experience.

When I got to married to Shalina, I was coming into her family as a divorced, white man with three kids; probably not in the family's grand plan for their daughter. Rather than reacting negatively to this, her mother Kiran was amazing. Her comment to her daughter was, 'Great, now you have a ready-made family.' Shalina was concerned that she didn't know the first thing about having a child. 'Well,' said her mother, 'don't worry. Mike does!'

I also had a former girlfriend who was Indian. Her parents would not even entertain the concept of a divorced person with kids marrying their daughter. I didn't even make it onto the radar, too much insult, the shame of it. That's not the basis of any relationship. Times change, but deep-rooted feelings often take longer to catch up.

## FAMILY BUSINESSES AND HOW TO SURVIVE THEM

The UK awnings and blinds manufacturer James Robertshaw was founded in 1860. A hundred years later, it was acquired from the Robertshaws by the father-in-law of the current MD,

Nigel Sharrock, who took over that role in the late 1970s: his wife and son are both on the board. The secret of the company's survival is, according to Nigel Sharrock, constant innovation, new machinery and business sense (all of course applicable to any successful business) – plus, significantly, 'family values'.

David Smith, professor of innovation management at Nottingham Business School, says, 'Quite often, businesses survive because they are family businesses. The family retains control and they don't sell out. The ones that do survive often have core values that are well established. They don't opt for sudden, short-term gains, and tend to take a long-term view of things.'

Those family values, and the closeness and understanding that drive a family business in the early years, can also be destructive. Roy Jacuzzi, who created the eponymous and ubiquitous whirlpool in the 1960s, brought his imagineering instincts into a family business founded by his grandfather's generation. In the late 1970s, the company was sold to the Kidde Corporation, by which time there were over 250 family members. Jacuzzi says: 'Can you imagine what the family organisation was like? When you start to get so many individuals and all of them have votes and different ideas, it gets to being a little bit gamey. It could be a zoo.'

*Family Business* magazine ran an analysis of family companies which had successfully survived for more than a hundred years, and identified a number of common features:

O  They remain small.

O  They keep ownership within the family.

O  They stay away from major cities.

O   They let a family member run the business.

Can these features apply to non-family businesses? They seem like nice-to-have rather than must-have options.

Perhaps these seven principles of building a family business from Forbes are more applicable. They were proposed by Fred Mouawad, whose family jewellery business, founded in 1891, is perhaps best known for its collaborations with Victoria's Secret. Fred is the fourth generation in the family business.

O   Courage

O   Discipline

O   Respect

O   Build into the future

O   Talent

O   Wisdom

O   Guardianship.

Now, those are some family characteristics to be proud of. I think most of them apply to every business, but the one I want to underline is the characteristic of 'guardianship'. We are all so caught up in day-to-day, minute-to-minute issues that demand our immediate response that we often forget to take the long view. Family businesses are constantly aware of the fact that the business will only continue to prosper if there is a clear line of succession.

What they must not forget is the 'family factor'. According to family business specialist Anita Brightley-Hodges, 'Aligning the values of the family with the business is the key to unlocking and resolving issues. Openness, collaboration, trust, flexibility, fairness, inclusivity, leadership, share of voice, truth, cohesion and communication are important in equal measure.'

Occasionally I see a commercial on the TV or in a magazine that really resonates with me. One I have always loved is the Patek Philippe watch advert: 'You never own a Patek Philippe. You merely look after it for the next generation.' Surely a great reminder of guardianship.

*'Guardianship is the mindset that you are the steward of the family enterprise till the next generation is readied for leadership. Guardianship is about taking the long-view. This is rare in a world where it is all about the fast exit.'*

Fred Mouawad

# IS BLOOD REALLY THICKER THAN WATER?

Promotion internally within any company is difficult. The same applies to a son, daughter or further-flung family member taking over from a parent in a family business. The most productive heir apparent may not be quite as apparent as strict primogeniture suggests.

Rupert Murdoch is having to come to terms with his succession. Having had something of a falling out with daughter Elizabeth, Rupert has placed his sons James and Lachlan in line to take over some, all, or none, of the multi-billion Murdoch empire. Like all families, they have had their fair share of rows and disagreements; it's just that the stakes are so much higher. Rupert still calls most of the shots, but he is obviously considering the succession. The *Financial Times* ran an article in 2017 about the two brothers, in which Rupert said, appreciatively, of Lachlan, 'He was always the most interested. When he was a 13-year-old kid, he worked as an apprentice in the pressroom, cleaning all the oil and grease off the press.'

Appointing a son or daughter to head up the company can have a negative effect on family ties. One retiring MD, whose son had taken over the business he had nurtured for years, said, 'I feel like our father–son relationship has been lost. I'm happy he has risen to the challenge and taken on the top job of the family business, but at what cost? We need help getting that balance back.'

Similarly, when a previous head of the family business can't quite let go, the effect is equally negative. When the next generation gamely tells everyone that they 'really welcome' their mother's or father's input and advice, the hidden message is that they actually know what they are doing and don't appreciate some old codger rocking up to tell them how it should be. They just want to get on with doing things their way, mistakes and all.

If two families live in the same village in India, all the kids play together in each other's houses, and everyone is Uncle or Auntie. They think of each other as their brothers, sisters and cousins, and before you know it they can barely distinguish between the ones who are genuine blood relatives and those who aren't.

In India, everyone is a cousin of someone. I recently went to the wedding of the children of two close family friends who are both powerful businessmen in the London hotel industry. The two families were marrying into each other. Shalina and I were there to witnesses this merging of two powerful families. The groom observed, 'Maybe I'm always going to be known as my father's son, but it makes you work harder to ensure you gain that respect among your fellow staff and family members.'

'Family' is a mutable concept. Blood ties often lead to feuds. Families without blood ties – where the children have been adopted, for example – are often as strong, if not stronger, because the desire to create a family has been so powerful. A friend of mine, who adopted his two children, says that his mother-in-law says that they are blessed, not because of their adoption, but because they have inherited none of her own family's genetic baggage.

I have another friend who has run a successful care-home business for thirty years, having built it up from nothing, owning all its real estate in the Brighton area. I met him recently and he told me he was getting planning permission to convert the entire portfolio to residential usage and then sell it off to developers. 'Why on earth would you do that?' I asked. He explained that, while the business had grown fabulously over the years and had provided him with a fantastic income for over two decades, he did not want to continue to manage it. His three daughters had all become successful within the medical profession and were not interested in taking over the business. So, instead of selling the business for the cash flow, he decided to sell the assets and capitalise on the accretion, and then sign up to the SKI (Spending the Kids' Inheritance) Club.

Are we obliged to adopt a route predefined by our parents? Can we be independent from their choices and still be respected by them? Of course. I watched a film on a flight from Bangkok to Hong Kong recently which included a great line used to talk down the chances of a particular colonel in the British army of being promoted. The line was, 'Sir, we shouldn't invite him to dine with us. He has had particular misfortune in choosing his ancestors.'

My father was not someone I was proud of at all. He was a wife beater and a criminal, and my siblings and I all rebelled against that by becoming members of the police force or the fire brigade, or successful in business. It could have been so different had we chosen to follow in his footsteps. So we should not be compelled to take on our parents' businesses if that is not what we get excited about. If we are to be truly successful in life, we need to be happy. It's difficult to see how we can be happy if we spend a third of our lives doing something we don't want to do.

I recently took delivery of a product from a company called 23andMe, a kit that allows you to analyse your genetic history by post. You register online and then mail out a saliva sample. Within a few weeks the results are accessible via the website. I have also used similar tools, such as iamYiam, which use genetic analysis to look for signs of hereditary medical issues and allergies, but this particular version was designed to highlight where in the world your ancestors came from. While for me there were no real surprises in terms of my genetic background, I do know that others have received some very unexpected results. It seems that we are all more integrated than we may realise.

In both families and business, the past has an impact on the future. We need to learn to channel this while also respecting the fact that the next generation will bring with them their own thinking. This next generation of super-tech-savvy kids has so much to offer to companies of all kinds. Families are changing and so must business; we can't let ingrained attitudes or cultures get in the way.

## QR: AUGMENTED DISCOVERY

Click on the QR code at the end of this chapter. You'll instantly download clips of me telling you more about each of these key points:

- Family businesses still represent – in the US and the UK – a significant percentage of SME companies operating in and contributing to the economy.

- The upsides of family businesses are understanding, resilience, trust and loyalty, and an emotional glue that can keep things together through crises.

- The flip sides of family businesses are that trust and loyalty can be betrayed and festering feuds follow. You can't resign from the family.

- Egos – especially autocratic father (or mother, but especially father) figures – are disruptive in the family and at work.

- Family is a mutable concept: the nuclear family has been exploded. There is no longer any 'normal' family. So let's use the positive values of family without being hung up by shape and form.

*'Families are from Venus, businesses from Mars.'*

Alan Barker

# Chapter 9

MT

WORK LIKE A FAMILY

# WORK LIKE A FAMILY

## We are family ...

*'Many a chairman will say he looks at his
company like family and then acts in a way
that makes you glad you're not related!'*

Richard Branson

I have always called my management team my 'family'. Whenever TelecityGroup acquired a company – there was a phase when I was overseeing its swift expansion and this was happening several times a year – my opening line to the new team joining the business was usually 'Welcome to the family.'

One day my wife and I were talking about some argument her own family were having. I said, 'I can't believe your family is bickering about this. You're lucky to have a family, because I don't really have a family per se.' And she said, 'Well, your team is your family.' And she meant it in a positive way, I think.

This was all about the fact that my family history had been, let's say, less than smooth. My father was one of nine children: both he and my mum were from large Irish families. Prior to the arrival of my stepbrother Anthony, a decade or so after me, I was the youngest of four, and my other siblings – two brothers and a sister – were all at least ten years older than me. We lived in various places in south-east London: Rotherhithe, Bermondsey, Lewisham.

My father was permanently renovating our houses. This meant I often came home to surprises: once there was no staircase left in the house, just a rope ladder to the first floor, which we had to climb to go to bed. Another time I found my mother in the kitchen perched on two planks of wood, cooking on a cooker that was precariously balanced on another couple of planks.

My father was an extremely jealous type. He had huge fights with anyone whom he imagined was looking at my mother. One bust-up with my grandfather was almost fatal: my father punched my grandad down the stairs, and in retaliation my grandad stabbed my dad in the street a week later. He lived to tell the tale: despite his 'issues', he was a survivor.

When I was seven my dad left home on a motorbike bound for Australia. I had been given the choice of staying with one parent or the other, an impossible decision for a seven-year-old. I chose my mother. She took me and one of my brothers to Rhodesia – this was long before Zimbabwe came into existence – to escape, but my father returned and tracked us down to our apartment in Salisbury. I have a powerful memory of my father trying to strangle my mother on the balcony, while she hit him with an iron to protect herself. He only stopped when she managed to murmur, 'Think of Michael.' Strange what power we have when we don't even know it. He was arrested and deported.

He came back again, in disguise and using a fake identity, but this time we had a tip-off he was coming and I remember being picked up from school in a chauffeured Jag (courtesy of my mother's boss) and being whisked off to the Umtali hills. My father eventually found us hiding away in a hotel out near the Mozambique border. He phoned the hotel room from a call box across the road. I remember looking out of the window and seeing him there, demanding to see me. After resisting for some time, my mother reluctantly relented and sent me down. I crossed the road and, as I approached him, he grabbed me by the collar and held me in front of the traffic, threatening to leave me in front of the next truck if my mother didn't come out of the hotel. Eventually she did. He cried and begged her to come back. He was arrested and deported again. I was eight years old.

That's why I told Shalina I don't really have a family. And yet I moved back to Rotherhithe recently, by sheer coincidence, choosing to set down roots some 50 metres from where it all began.

## A FAMILY OF SHARED VALUES

Perhaps the truth is that 'family' is more about a sense of shared values than shared blood.

I have a friend, an acquaintance maybe – I'm not entirely sure where the dividing line technically lies – who lives in Washington DC but also has a house in London. We have met on and off over the years, through business, in various places around the world. Whenever we meet we immediately establish empathy.

I called him out of the blue one day to see how he was and he said, 'I'm in London': he's rarely there, so I proposed we get together for a drink. Just before we were meant to meet at a café in Kensington, he texted and suggested I pop across to his London house instead. 'It's just around the corner,' he said, 'and it will save me coming out, plus we have friends who have come round.'

I went over to his place, a gorgeous house, with lovely high ceilings, which was a hive of activity: his kids were skateboarding back and forth all around me. The friends who were visiting him, it turned out, were also in the same kind of business, and because of the homely, family feel at the house we became 'good friends in the inner circle' and went on to do business together. At one level that was smart networking, but looking back I realise he wouldn't have invited me in if we hadn't already had a positive relationship. That 'family' environment fostered an openness and immediate trust, a kind of naturally supportive network.

Paralympian Richard Whitehead has talked about the importance of support in his own life. 'Earlier on in my life it was all about getting through childhood, dealing with these physical and social barriers, overcoming lots of knockbacks. But I always had that support network of a family telling me there would always be an opportunity for me in life: what was important was how I decided to embrace it.'

## FAMILY INC.

The Australian economist Joshua Gans once decided to try applying the economic principles he has developed, especially around incentives, to parenting. There were some unexpected side-effects. For example, one young girl brought in to toilet-train a younger sibling discovered that – since there was a reward for each success – she could fill her younger brother up with excessive amounts of water to increase the number of rewards she received.

In a similar vein, a *Wall Street Journal* article, 'Run Your Family Like a Business', explored the application of business ideas to family life, following one family who had brought into their home a regime of accountability checklists, mission statements, conflict resolution techniques and chore rotas. They swore it had improved the dynamic of the family and made communication far better.

These are just two examples of how traditional business ideas have been deployed in a domestic setting. However, I am not convinced that this is necessarily the best direction of flow. Wouldn't it be more valuable to see which lessons from family life could improve working relationships?

Rather than treating your family like a business, I would prefer to invert the whole idea. I believe business should be viewed more as a family – both in more formal ways, like the organisational structure (working in small teams, for example), as well as with regard to the positive, more qualitative elements: caring for each other, celebrating, sharing fun, giving praise not criticism, impromptu communication.

The fact that those qualities often seem alien to the workspace merely underlines the way we naturally tend to view work and life as separate entities. What is the difference between kids seeking attention and colleagues at work doing the same? If someone comes into the office throwing his teddy out of the pram, storming around, threatening to leave, we naturally say, 'Sit down and tell me about this.' At home, we have a completely different attitude.

Just as we need to learn afresh how we behave at work, we also have to understand our staff. They are not robots or apparatchiks: they are human beings, individuals, who bring to work their own problems and attitudes, learnt or influenced as children within their own families and through their own experiences.

Most of us will recognise what is known as 'transference', where grown-ups relate to other grown-ups as if they were authority figures from their childhood, figures who could be their parents, their teachers or older brothers or sisters. When they apply that thinking to their relationship with their line manager or boss, this can lead to problems. But that doesn't mean that we shouldn't allow and encourage everyone in organisations to speak up openly when something is troubling them, as you might do to a family member.

Generation Y staff and millennials have often been raised in far less traditional family structures, in single-parent families, with complex sibling and half-sibling relationships. This is what they bring into the workplace. So if you are going to treat your staff as family – as I like to do – you have to be prepared to think outside your own experience of 'family' and embrace all of its possibilities. This can be challenging.

Beyond Generation Y there is now Generation C, driven by creation, curation, connectivity and community, defined by behaviour and not by age. When they are not working, shopping or banking online, they are on social media. Generation C will judge your organisation by its website, its Twitter, Facebook and Instagram presence, not by a sumptuously printed glossy brochure. Just as families continue to evolve, so do the people you work with. Take the time to understand everyone at work, whatever age they are and wherever they come from. Treating them all with respect and empathy is simply good business sense.

## A PROBLEM SHARED...

So yes, treat your company as a family in search of a freer, more fluid, more flexible business dynamic. But, because you will be giving up the safety net apparently offered by old-style business relationships determined by hierarchical organigrams and rigid job descriptions, you must be prepared to deal with all the problems that come with being part of a family. And, as we know, 'all families are dysfunctional', or, as the novelist Douglas Coupland put it more pungently, 'All families are psychotic.'

The quality and the stability of life outside work inevitably have an impact on what happens in work. Many companies expect their staff to have the capacity to sort out their own problems by themselves and not bring them into the workplace. I think we should positively encourage those problems to be aired – if appropriate – so that leaders at work can provide help in a caring, but also dispassionate, way.

How many of us know the pain experienced by our colleagues? Should we feel their pain? Can we be of value, be a sounding board for colleagues' sadness or confusion? It takes a lot for staff to open up at work, so (if and when they do), they need to be treated with patience and imagination.

One of the single most important things I did when I was leading TelecityGroup was to take individual country managers out for dinner on a regular basis. I would fly in the night before a review meeting, and the country manager and I would go to a restaurant. Over the course of a meal and a few drinks, we would not talk about the business at all, but about their personal lives: how their relationships were going, how their kids were getting on at school, any health concerns they might have.

The managers used to tell me that they valued this time

more than any other. It gave them a chance to pour out any issues that were troubling them without feeling they were being judged or assessed. Of course, from my perspective, it was also an opportunity to understand how much stress they might be under. These sessions also gave me a sense of how far I could stretch and push them from a business point of view to get the maximum effort out of them, without tipping them over the edge.

It's a tradition I have continued as a non-executive chairman. I know from my own experience that the role of the CEO is often a lonely one, with no one there to help shoulder the responsibility for performance, good or bad, or to bounce ideas off. In board meetings where other directors and maybe shareholders are present, it is difficult for CEOs to open up. The agenda is too complex, too nuanced. Generally they veer to the defensive, which is not useful. That is where a good chairman can earn his or her weight in gold. I regularly invite the CEOs to dinner for off-site meetings. They seem to open up more and share their innermost feelings and concerns.

There are similarities at home. I have learnt that my wife is also my best friend, and we regularly organise date nights, where we can go out for a meal and discuss anything that we might not yet have had the opportunity to talk about because of the pressures and hassles of daily life. It helps to know that someone else is aware of the issues you are thinking and worrying about. Even if they are not in a position to give any specific or practical help, it is reassuring to know they understand, and the act of listening and sharing is a boon.

Steve, the site manager who did a fantastic job of rebuilding my house, is an amazing guy. On the outside you'd think he was a real East End bruiser, but for those who get to know him he is a total softie. His wife is the only person who can boss him around. When he was on site, he would sometimes explode and get incredibly angry – in person or on the phone – with contractors or labourers who had done something wrong or failed to show up on time.

At one point I said, 'Steve, slow down. Relax. You are going to have a heart attack. It's a job. Your bosses are not going to thank you for it when you go off sick through stress. When you are lying in hospital, they are not going to remember the twenty years of your temples throbbing.' It's at times like this that we all need someone to talk to and understand our frustrations, whether that's work colleagues, or family, or both. Sharing is an important part of both work and family life and a key aspect of better work/life integration.

## THE FAMILY OF STAKEHOLDERS

I have already talked about the fact that the largest stakeholder in 'YOU The Business' is your family. They rely on your income, not just financial but emotional.

When families implode, or explode, there are major implications. A report cited by Oliver James, based on interviews with 8,000 mothers following a separation, divorce or break-up, revealed that mothers were more likely to be more depressed after a year alone than when they were in a relationship, even if their relationship had been really bad prior to separation. Perhaps that's why we often have 'rebound' relationships immediately after a break-up. They may not last, but they're better than being alone.

That's why I believe that symbols of a relationship are so important: to remind ourselves of the fact that we are part of a bigger team. I wear a chain with a silver symbol. It reflects the fact that, following my divorce, Shalina took a huge leap of faith to marry me. And I was still insecure. An engagement ring is a symbol, a demonstration of a commitment. Because men generally don't wear engagement rings, Shalina bought me a necklace, which matches my wedding ring, as my equivalent of an engagement ring. I have never taken the necklace off since. It has a very unusual design, which often prompts people who meet me to ask about it. That in turn gives me the opportunity to tell them the whole story behind it, which I love.

It's a statement, like having a tattoo. I talked to Richard Whitehead about the tattoo on his arm: 'Cometh the hour, cometh the man'. For him, it's a message about 'stepping up to the plate, learning from experience and that knowledge is power. Whether it's academically or through life experiences the ability to learn from other people and then utilise that messaging for yourself is a powerful thing.' It is also a permanent reminder that allows Richard to 'look back at a time in my life when I wasn't running or doing sport, and the life change that I had to make, grasping the opportunity to better myself'. And, like my wedding necklace, it's a good prompt for starting a conversation.

## A LITTLE CHAT GOES A LONG WAY

Communication is vital. We love to make new friends socially. Being invited to dinner parties where we might know some, but not all, of the other guests is a fantastic way to meet new people in a relatively 'safe' environment. You can explore a conversation with someone and, if it takes an awkward turn, or if you feel there is not the right chemistry between you, there are other friends in the room to retreat to.

This works in a business environment as well. I go to

dozens of drinks receptions every year, at least one a week. I am bound to know people there, but I will most likely meet people I don't know, and having an interesting topic to break the ice is so important.

Sometimes there are days when I don't feel like engaging with people. My wife often asks me why I go to so many networking events when I am exhausted or have little free time, but she also understands that some of these chance meetings turn into business in the future, sometimes even years into the future.

Most of my strong business relationships end up being personal friendships. It's a fine line to balance business with friendship, but I have not found it to be difficult. If you are always conscious of conducting business with integrity, you should have nothing to fear when it comes to doing business with friends. Equally, recognising that humans are fallible and make mistakes is important. It allows you to be 'authentic' and be yourself. So what if you say something wrong? If it is done with good intentions, it will soon be forgotten.

I once heard an interview with an entrepreneur who was asked the age-old question, 'What is the secret of your success?' He replied, 'Two words: good choices.' The reporter asked a follow-up question, 'Ah, OK, so how do you always make good choices?' This time the response was 'One word: experience.' A little frustrated, the reporter pushed the point. 'And how do you get the experience?' The entrepreneur didn't hesitate. 'Two words: bad choices!'

And that, in theory, is the case with family. As long as you remain true to your principles and apply integrity to your actions and decisions, doing business with family should be straightforward.

A couple of years ago I took my family to Istanbul on

holiday. The first morning we were there everyone wanted a relaxed start to the vacation, so I planned a board meeting with my Turkish subsidiary starting at 7 am. I rented a meeting room in our hotel, held the board meeting and was back in the room before everyone was ready to come down for breakfast. It was easy to integrate business and family life there. Moreover, one of the board members had a stake in a helicopter charter company and when he found out we were there on vacation he organised for me and the family to be flown around Istanbul, skimming between Asia and Europe across the Bosphorus. In this case, integrating the board meeting into our holiday not only did not have a negative impact on the family vacation, but it actually enhanced it.

Today some of my best friends are as close as any family can be. And most of those friendships have evolved out of business relationships. I was even introduced to my wife Shalina by her cousin Sheetal, who was on the board of a company with me. So clearly my business relationship with him had become strong enough that he had the confidence to introduce me to his cousin and effectively 'turn me into family'.

Incidentally, when I first met Shalina, Sheetal introduced me to her during a charity ball where I was conducting the auction alongside another good friend, the newscaster Alastair Stewart. Shalina and I exchanged a handful of words during a 20-second period and, as I subsequently discovered, she had an immediate dislike for me. She thought that I was a bad lad, and she was probably right. It was not the best chapter of my life. I subsequently made consistent attempts to contact her, but all of them failed. Over a whole year I kept trying, with not so much as a returned call or email. Then, luckily for me, Sheetal intervened and tried again. He invited me to Shalina's birthday party and this time we hit it off straight away. We were engaged a few months later.

So it seems that, like business, personal life is about persistence, luck and timing. But that business relationship with Sheetal was more than simply business, and the friendship was something far more valuable than a business contact. It has provided me with a lifetime of happiness.

It is always worth building relationships at work in the same way as you would in your private life. It creates a kind of business family.

## QR: AUGMENTED DISCOVERY

Click on the QR code opposite. You'll instantly download clips of me telling you more about each of these key points:

- It is more effective to apply family values in business than vice versa. The idea of applying spreadsheets and checklists to family life is the wrong way round.

- The relationships between work colleagues often mirror the relationships within the family. Resolving conflicts and misunderstandings requires the same openness and communication that creates a well-balanced family environment.

- Given the growing integration of work and life, problems and issues outside work will inevitably spill over into work. Listening to and supporting colleagues at these times has a beneficial impact on productivity.

*'If you want your children to be more intelligent, read them more fairy tales.'*

Albert Einstein

# Part IV

# PROSPER

# Chapter 10

# PROSPER TOGETHER

## Success doesn't mean you have to be a robot

*'We don't stop playing because we get old.*
*We get old because we stop playing.'*

George Bernard Shaw

We are all only human; that is a truth we sometimes forget. Vulnerability is not something that leaders often exhibit – at least, not voluntarily – probably because it is usually perceived as a sign of weakness.

In reality, the opposite is true. Vulnerability is a strength. But to show vulnerability you need inner confidence and a high level of self-awareness. The counterpart of vulnerability is the ability to demonstrate and share kindness. Like love, these might seem alien concepts in business.

It's like the skill of listening. Don Draper in *Mad Men* put it like this: 'People want to be told what to do so badly that they'll listen to anyone.' But what might have been true in the 1960s is no longer relevant.

There have been significant changes in attitude, in both consumer industries and the corporate business world, about how the behaviour of an organisation, and how it is perceived to behave, directly influences how clients, customers and consumers feel and behave towards that business.

Corporate social responsibility has become a much more widely understood and accepted concept, embraced by companies large and small. The issue has become more pertinent recently since the arrival and growth of social media, and, in particular, the rise and rise of Twitter, Facebook and YouTube.

Sharing is the new caring, whether that's Airbnb, on course to take over from the long-established hotel groups; BlaBlaCar, allowing a more efficient use of cars; or shared spaces for 'at home' workers to operate together and enjoy the benefits of office culture.

Social media is changing the way we think, feel and react to corporates, who were once able to exercise strict control over what information they released. During the Gulf oil spill of 2010, the Twitter feed @BPGlobalPR had 190,000 followers; BP's official feed had just 18,000.

None of us has genuine relationships with a thousand people, yet many Facebook or LinkedIn users have a thousand 'friends' or contacts. I use LinkedIn as a way of keeping in touch with people's news, ideas and progress. I may never contact them, but if I've met someone, taken their business card and connected with them on LinkedIn, then I can find them instantly, even if they change jobs.

I used to spend a lot of time assessing the value of people I met, calculating what they could bring to me, rather than what I could offer them. I've learnt that inverting that equation actually brings long-term benefits that you can't possibly know at the time.

After I published *Forget Strategy. Get Results*, I was

contacted by someone called Stephen Murphy, who said he had enjoyed the book and asked me to come over to the London offices of his company, DJO Global, to give a talk to his management team of fifteen or so people. I headed over there a few weeks later.

It turned out that Stephen – who, like me, is a frequent traveller – was reading an article in an in-flight magazine that referenced my first book. Stephen says:

*I made a note and ordered the book. I liked it so much I ordered another 20 copies to give to all my direct reports. I liked Michael's backstory. The title was catchy. The messages were relevant. I didn't agree with it all, but I liked Mike's different approach. I hadn't done anything as extreme as the trips to the Ice Hotel or swimming with sharks that Michael has put together for his management team, but I had organised events I considered extreme: various rock-climbing events, white-water rafting and camping. A US company is always very keen on health and safety, so the sharks were out.*

Stephen had paired off his managers, and each pair took one of the chapters in the book – Faith or Failure or Fear, for example. One of the pair had to argue for a positive view of my chapter, while the other took an opposite position. While they were doing their preparation, he hadn't told them I was going to be there to judge their take on my book: 'I kept the fact that Michael would be coming to the session top secret: only I and my secretary knew. When I kicked off the session and told the team that Michael Tobin himself would be adjudicating the event, a couple of them sat up – some clearly hadn't done much preparation.'

It was fascinating for me to hear their interpretations of what I had written.

Stephen heard about my plan to run 40 marathons in 40 days and got back in touch again. He asked me if I knew what DJO Global did – and to my chagrin I had to admit that I didn't. I had shot into the presentation with virtually no preparation, knowing that it was about my book, which I knew inside out. They had done their research on me far better than I had on them.

DJO Global, it turned out, make high-end technology for elite athletes, such as Tour de France cyclists, to aid rapid overnight recovery. Stephen said he would like to donate some equipment for me to use during the marathons. It was invaluable. I used it every one of those 40 days – and afterwards – to help me recover.

Stephen reported back that 'for the sales team the fact that Michael used our products for the 40 marathons in 40 days meant a lot. That engagement is not something that can be learnt, it comes from the heart.'

DJO Global are in the healthcare business; they understand that the technology is, for them, a tool. As Stephen explains:

*Talking to customers, some are fascinated by technological innovation – they love that level of detail – but others are simply turned off by it. You need to understand those relationships, and thinking about the other person's frame of reference, likes and dislikes, is really important. An overemphasis on technology can impair or water down a relationship. It's often better to sit down, have lunch. The value of that can be much higher. Sending an email or a text does not mean you have done your job. It's about keeping it personal, not generic. Walking the floor, shaking hands.*

Stephen gives an example from his own family life.

*My son did a placement in one of our overseas offices. He*

*gave me some feedback from a member of staff there who complimented me on my leadership, not because I was super fair or had given her a pay rise, but because whenever I visited their offices and walked through the building, I remembered her name and asked about her son. In head offices, especially in North America, there are too many offices with closed doors. No one is walking the floor, they have forgotten about the one-on-one relationships.*

## TECHNOLOGY WITH EMPATHY

In 2012, a poll found that the brand attributes that consumers found most important were – yes – 'kindness and empathy', and a friendly and socially responsible attitude. A non-empathetic habit we are getting into is turning nouns into verbs: I am going to train it home. Shall we Uber it back? And I wonder if that is a reflection of some sort of alienation.

One thing that concerns me, as it seems to negate empathy, is the use of devices such as Amazon Echo. There are many in the marketplace. I have the Echo all over my house with its little 'repeater' device The Dot. I have it integrated into my home automation. Alexa is the 'name' we use to grab the attention of the device. 'Hey Alexa, open the curtains,' 'Hey Alexa, turn off the lights,' 'Hey Alexa, put on my favourite playlist.'

It strikes me that the next generation is growing up with these devices, where orders are blurted out without courtesy and carried out as a servant would obey a master. This is very concerning to me. I am a great fan and advocate of technology, and voice recognition and augmented reality is definitely the way forward, but how about if we programmed our devices only to accept the commands with a 'Please' at the beginning and a 'Thank you' at the end? Would that be such a hardship? Would it not contribute to a better social dynamic if our children were not growing up barking commands and getting angry when they are not immediately obeyed?

Microsoft recently ran a test in which they equipped a device with Intelligent Response technology using machine learning to adapt its 'nature' according to its surroundings. The device was effectively a chatbot. Listening to comments and responding to them, it also learnt what people were saying and tried to 'evolve' its character to align with the community it was interacting with. This is in many ways what we do subconsciously every day, but more quickly and more accurately. Microsoft had to take down the system after 48 hours, as it had become racist. The technology was trying to empathise with its interlocutors but had lost its moral compass. Could this explain some of the results we have seen in global democracy recently? Have politicians resorted to machine learning and forgotten their own reasons for wanting to be in politics?

And, indeed, do we care? Are we, as recipients of this phenomenon, becoming 'used' to it, or even more accepting of it?

Consider the oDesk software that allows a boss to monitor the staff working from home by watching them via their own computer's webcam, and even detecting their keystrokes. Efficient, in tune with the outsourcing of staff, but scarily Big Brother.

Consider, too, the softer side of monitoring technology. Rather than watching and spying, CCTV cameras are being used in Cambridge to help older people stay in their own homes rather than moving to care homes, preserving their independence for as long as possible – clearly a major issue as the population ages. The CCTV cameras have additional abilities, able to analyse body temperatures and pulse rates and monitor muscle twitch. So, if your grandmother or grandfather is unwell but not aware of the danger, the system is able to alert relatives and doctors to provide early help, a positive benefit rather than an intrusion.

Yet, like the idea of microchipping yourself, the knee-jerk reaction is that there is far too much personal data being shared with third parties, and that these ideas are an invasion of privacy.

But that is not the fault of technology. The tech is simply a tool. It is the exploiters of the tool whom we need to fear. There is nothing new about that concept. In Stone Age times a bone on the ground was simply that: a bone. But in the hands of an angry caveman, it became a weapon of choice.

At some point in the not-too-distant future we will be reading about a driverless car consciously taking the decision to run over an elderly person and we will be horrified. In reality, machine learning will have evolved so far that we will then discover that the car was given a choice of either hitting a five-year-old child on one side of the road or swerving and hitting the pensioner.

The car will consciously have made the decision that a child, having an average of 95.6 years of life ahead of it, would be more valuable to protect for society than a great-grandfather with perhaps three years of life left. That is a terrible thought, isn't it? But why is that? In the absence of any other data on the two individuals concerned, what would we as a human driver do in those circumstances? Would we even make a decision? Would we be able to live with ourselves even if we did have the split-second reaction time to decide on something like that?

I would imagine our own self-preservation instincts would come into play and we would try to avoid killing ourselves before even reflecting on the long-term outcome of our actions.

So the computer now positively chooses to take the life of a human. Have we passed the ultimate taboo? Can we get our minds around that? If you were forced to choose in the above scenario and had the reaction times to reflect and make the choice, wouldn't you do the same?

Imagine a health service in twenty years' time that, under pressure of budgets and a growing, and ageing, population, starts to run algorithms to allocate resources, effectively choosing who lives and dies.

To a certain extent humankind does that already. In the theatres of war that occur around the world, medics use triage to prioritise injured service personnel in real-time situations according to their ability to make a difference or to keep them alive. The postcode lottery is a version of that based simply on where you are born. And private healthcare is a way for individuals who can afford it to choose to preserve themselves and their loved ones with a higher percentage chance of survival that the vast majority of the developing world.

Robotic and machine learning is evolving at unprecedented speed. When they become 'superhuman' we may be quite content that the machine or the robot will make the tough decisions for us, absolving us of the guilt of having to do it ourselves. So perhaps a guilt-free existence is one of the ultimate emotions we will be able to experience. Do we aspire to benefit from the attributes of robots?

In fact, is technology the problem here, or is it that it merely brings to the fore deeper issues and concerns in our own psyche that trouble us and which we do not wish to confront? In which case, it is much easier to blame technology.

## LIFE WITH NO LIMITS

As mentioned earlier, I have observed over time that in youth we spend all our time trying to create wealth and in our latter years we spend all of our wealth trying to create more time.

The amazing Steve Jobs reserved this nugget for his last recorded words:

*Non-stop pursuing of wealth will only turn a person into a twisted being, just like me. Love can travel a thousand miles. Life has no limit. Go where you want to go. Reach the height you want to reach. It is all in your heart and in your hands. What is the most expensive bed in the world? – 'Sickbed'… You can employ someone to drive the car for you, make money for you but you cannot have someone to bear the sickness for you. Whichever stage in life we are at right now, with time, we will face the day when the curtain comes down. Treasure love for your family, love for your spouse, love for your friends.*

I cry each time I read this. The message is simple. I agree with it. I even preach it. But I find myself constantly contradicting it. Here I am crying writing this now.

How often do we ignore the few people who are going to be there on that dreaded day. The day we say goodbye to all our social media followers, the day we give away everything we have worked for, the day that the world begins to forget we existed. That day, if we are really lucky, there will be a few individuals, loved ones, who will feel they want to spend those precious moments with us. Those last seconds.

As you are reading this, you know who these people are. Can you honestly say that you have treated them well enough that they will move heaven and earth to be there for that moment? Not only for your sake, but for theirs? I truly hope you can.

## UNDERSTANDING OTHER PEOPLE'S POINTS OF VIEW

Adopting a more sharing and caring attitude in business is also about understanding other people's points of view.

If you can identify your own, often unconscious, biases, you can compensate for them or at least be aware of them. In an increasingly collegiate world, all of us are going to have our own biases. So think about approaching situations with an open attitude: 'I have this particular opinion – and opinions are good, it's far better to have an opinion than to prevaricate – but equally I am aware that I am approaching this from my own angle, and someone else might offer a better position or help me refine my opinion for the better.'

Research has shown that people are interested in fairness; the process leading to an outcome can be as important as (if not more important than) the outcome itself.

Here are some ways to help create a fair workplace:

O Engage people in decision-making by asking for their ideas and encouraging them to challenge proposals. People need to feel confident that their voice is being heard.

O Explain the thinking behind the final decision. People must feel you have been candid for them to trust your intentions, especially if their ideas have not been accepted.

O Set clear expectations and state the rules of the game, including performance standards. Communicate what you believe the outcomes are likely to be or what you expect them to be.

We don't need to be anti-art to be a scientist: in other words, you don't always have to have a contrary position simply because it is good to have a contrary position. And if someone else comes up with an idea, approach it with the view, how do I make that work, as opposed to why won't it work?

Why is our political system structured as Government and Opposition? It is supremely important that any government is tested and challenged. A majority still has to allow for the opinions of the minority. But it seems as though our parties are set up more for opposing what the other thinks than finding ways to progress as a culture and a community.

Understanding other people's points of view is part of nurturing long-term relationships. Politicians are generally, though not exclusively, tough characters who are resilient to criticism, but seem less and less a source of inspiration for the community. Entrepreneurs need nurturing and sheltering and caring for. They are not hard-ass people, not business people. They are a great source of inspiration and ideas, but often useless at getting them to happen.

I would describe myself as a capitalist by day and a socialist by night. I want to make money. I want to create wealth. After all, taxes can only be taken if people are earning. But we live in a responsible world. So looking after people who are less fortunate that ourselves is vital.

My mantra is 'respect everyone, hurt no one and regret nothing'. People often say to me that the problem is that, as a principle, it doesn't work to its extreme. If you regret nothing, you may hurt someone, and if you are focused only on respect, perhaps you will miss an opportunity to create value that you would regret. I say that respecting everyone is a minimum requirement in life. Hurting no one is a little trickier. But if you are honest, even though in the short term the truth might hurt, it is always the right thing to do. And regretting nothing... Most elderly people on their deathbeds regret what they didn't do, not what they did do, which for me means we should 'just do it'.

I feel extremely lucky to have wound up where I am in life. And yes, success and good fortune are largely luck. Let no one tell you otherwise. That is why I am the socialist at night. It is important to me to give back to society, especially to create opportunities for the young and underprivileged. But taxes generally frustrate me. If I had my way, I would lower income tax and increase VAT. Value Added Tax is a luxury tax that can be imposed when people spend money on things that are luxuries. I want to encourage people to create value, but ensure that those who choose to live with a degree of 'luxury' pay more. A lot more.

I am on planes frequently, probably more frequently than I would ideally like. Before every takeoff come the flight safety announcements. And, regardless of the airline, they all say the same thing: 'In the event of an emergency, oxygen masks will fall from the compartments above.' And then, 'Make sure you fit your own mask properly before attempting to help others.' That is because, if you try to help a child sitting next to you, for example, which is indeed a natural reaction, they may be panicking, twisting and turning, and before you know it you will be out of oxygen and then there will be two people at risk. Sort yourself out and then help others. But above all don't forget to help those others.

Humankind has prospered because it has worked together. It may be competitive within the species but it always works for the common good. Business should and must be like this. If there is no win–win, then there is no win.

## QR: AUGMENTED DISCOVERY

Click on the QR code opposite. You'll instantly download clips of me telling you more about each of these key points:

- Simple, easy-to-implement activities – sharing a thank-you message to one colleague every day, for example – have an uplifting effect. I call this 'viral happiness'.

- Demonstrating vulnerability is not a sign of weakness. Being prepared to show vulnerability requires a high level of inner confidence and self-awareness.

- Our behaviour – not only to colleagues, but beyond, to clients, suppliers and customers – directly affects how our business is perceived.

- The perception of our business – particularly of the value of fairness – is boosted by engagement, explanation of intentions and clear expectations.

- If you want to make your dreams come true, STAY AWAKE.

*'Everyone thinks of changing the world, but no one thinks of changing himself.'*

Leo Tolstoy

MT

PROSPER TOGETHER

# Chapter 11

# PROSPER ORGANICALLY

## There is no quick-fix solution

*'If you want a long-term relationship that doesn't require a lot of work, I say, Get a dog. They love you no matter what. But when it comes to humans, there's no secret: you really have to appreciate the person every single day.'*

Denis Leary

If your business, or your family, is going to stay together, evolve together and prosper together, then a vision of the long term is vital. If the short term dominates, then the seesaw of emotions and cobbled-together solutions can be destructive. Many wealthy families have destroyed themselves because they have allowed fluctuating emotions to get in the way of a longer-term vision.

Prosperity in material terms can be destructive – although it doesn't have to be. Are there lessons to be learnt from those who have achieved what is defined as wealth? The kind of wealth that allows you to buy an island in the Caribbean, have a private jet on permanent standby, insulate (or isolate) yourself from real life?

The website Quora asked those questions. The respondees included Carol Philo, whose poverty-stricken parents became millionaires when a printing company they owned and ran out of the family's spare bedroom took off. With the profit, came an obsession for more and more wealth. According to Carol, they became 'addicted to the money. Nothing was ever enough.'

A similar viewpoint came from Murat Morrison, who sold out his trucking company in the late 1990s. 'Money buys comfort,' Morrison said. 'Comfort is not happiness or satisfaction. I felt as empty as a drum for the next few years. While it is good to be comfortable it is more satisfying to be happy.'

Another respondent reflected on the reactions of other people to perceived prosperity: 'Since most people imagine being rich as nirvana, you are no longer allowed to have any human needs or frustrations in the public eye. Yet, you are still a human being, but most people don't treat you like one.'

It's a double-edged sword. Material prosperity gives you freedom to do things you couldn't otherwise achieve, to have fresh experiences, to help other people.

The only problem is that contentment and happiness are not as measurable as a bank account. In 1968, Robert Kennedy said of the GDP measurement of a nation's prosperity, 'it measures everything, except that which makes life worthwhile'.

Integrated prosperity requires a broader view of what wealth is, and how external and internal wealth can co-exist.

## WEALTH AND WELL-TH

A fresh approach to prosperity within business demands that long-term vision overrides short-term gains. Here are some examples.

## DON'T HIRE THE BEST TECHNICAL PEOPLE...

... unless they're flexible and interested in lifetime learning. If you hire someone with several degrees, those credentials are probably going to be an important source of identity for that person. Will they be prepared to branch out from what they know? Hire people who are adaptable and interested in continuous learning. Give me someone who lacks skills but has the right attitude every time over someone who has the skills but the wrong attitude.

Towards the end of 2006, I was attempting to recruit a head of media for TelecityGroup. The final choice came down to two candidates: one already had the right experience and credentials, the other was a project manager from Cable & Wireless. For the job itself I went with the candidate who had the media experience. At the time the business was still in recovery mode and we could not afford the luxury of making errors of judgement in our recruiting. However, I had really enjoyed meeting Rob, the guy from Cable & Wireless, liked him, and didn't want to lose the opportunity to work with him. I always recruit on my gut instinct and there was something about him...

Although I could not offer Rob the media position, I got back to him and said, 'Rob, I really like you. You haven't got the head of media job, but I would still like you to come and work for me.' 'Doing what?' he asked. 'I don't know,' I said.

Rob was puzzled. 'So you're saying you want me to commit to working with you: leaving a well-established company for a small private one, for about the same money, but with at least two hours a day extra commuting – and you can't actually tell me the job I will be doing?' 'That's right,' I replied. 'Sorry, Mike,' Rob said. 'It's too vague; it's not for me.'

I was still determined to keep him involved. 'I tell you what, come and join us at our Christmas party on Thursday. Meet the rest of the team. I won't tell them why you there – I'll just introduce you as my friend.'

Rob agreed to come along to the Christmas do. It was at the Asia De Cuba Restaurant on St Martin's Lane in London. All my country managers from around Europe were there, plus my head office management team. We had drinks and dinner, laughed a lot, and Rob chatted away with the team. I didn't even get to speak to him the whole evening until it was time to say goodnight around midnight. The next morning he called me up. 'I have no idea why I am saying this, but having talked to the guys last night, I am going to say "yes".'

When Rob joined in the New Year, I started him off looking at our internal networks, but at the end of February, just as we were getting ready to press the button for our IPO that October, I asked to have a word with him. 'Rob, I'd like you to stop what you are doing and run this IPO process for me.'

This time he was not just puzzled, he was completely shocked. 'Are you crazy? I'm a project manager from a technical company. I'm an engineer who knows nothing about investors, financing or IPOs, and you want me to handle the most important event in Telecity's history in the middle of an economic crisis?' 'Yep.' Still shaking his head, Rob accepted. That was his leap of faith.

I was delighted, because I knew that with Rob's logical, questioning engineering brain and his lack of directly relevant experience – and precisely because of that lack of experience – he would go through every single aspect and detail of the IPO, querying everything, discovering the negatives, solving them, and that he would make it happen. He did a truly amazing job. Citibank and Deutsche Bank both told me that in their experience it was one of the smoothest, slickest IPOs they had ever been involved in. And that was run by a man who had no prior IPO experience. Rob learnt so much from that year that I made him first the temporary head of investor relations and then the chief operating officer of the whole company.

## DON'T USE PERFORMANCE FOR MANAGEMENT SELECTION...

... unless the old job is related to the new one. People who are good at what they do are often promoted into a managerial role that requires different and unfamiliar skills. Instead, create a dual promotion track for experts and managers.

I always pick managers based on their ability to understand the vision. The fact that they can see where the business needs to be heading is infinitely more valuable than a specific skill set. Also I do not like to refer to them as 'managers', and I avoid that term in their job titles. Your job as a leader is simply to create more leaders. That's it. Nothing more. So having someone inspirational who can take his or her team through uncharted territory and focus on the vision is gold dust. Skill sets are ten a penny. Leadership is rare and so, so valuable.

## DON'T MAKE GENERALISATIONS ABOUT GENERATIONS...

... unless you understand that all generalisations fail at the individual level. Get to know your people. You'll get the best out of your teams if you understand their specific traits and treat them as individuals.

How many times have we made references to people based on a specific attribute? Let's not refer to sexism, racism or ageism, but imagine this: you are walking down the street, and coming towards you are five punk rockers with safety pins in their noses, leather jackets over their hoodies. I bet your instant reaction with this image in your mind is 'Uh oh, trouble ahead, cross the road.' Notice there was no specificity of gender, race or age in my description, just style, yet it evokes a prejudice. We are all prejudiced to one degree or another. And this is a 'safety' mechanism that is very valuable to us, created from our past experiences. It is designed to protect us and enhance our judgement. But we need to be very careful to understand the difference between experience and indoctrination. We need to balance trusting our own judgement with not judging a book by its cover (including this one!).

## DON'T SURROUND YOURSELF WITH PEOPLE LIKE YOURSELF...

... unless you're looking for groupthink. Learn the value of others who are not like you, people who may actually make you feel a little uncomfortable and who bring a different perspective.

Diversity is extremely important, both in business and in the way we think and live. We must recognise that the truth in any situation can be different for different people according to their point of view. And it is exactly that diversity that we should look to capture, especially in business.

I once gave a keynote speech to a woman-in-business organisation in the ballroom of Claridge's. I was one of two men in the room with around 400 women. My speech was supposed to kick off a debate about women on PLC boards.

My opening line was, 'Men and women are not the same...' The place erupted. I didn't have chance to finish even the first sentence of my speech before I was looking for the emergency exits. What I had been planning to say was that if men and women were the same, how could we possibly fight for a balance on boards. Men and women are different and that is exactly the reason why boards should be diverse. If men and women were the same, what argument would there be for diversity on boards as a value proposition?

The key is that different characters are good for development. For business and for personal life, surrounding yourself with different opinions and being open to them is powerful. It can enhance and change your experience and endorse your conviction.

Let me give you a couple of examples of how those differences can be beneficial.

Anthony Morris has known me for over thirty years: he is a genuine Renaissance man – at one time a professional French horn player, now a composer and writer, who has lived, worked and studied in Europe, and has, variously, run a fax and telex bureau, sold the occasional computer, and worked in events management, broadcast consultancy and equipment development.

We first met sometime in the late 1980s. Anthony had received an enquiry from one of his clients for a specific model of portable computer; I was then the French computer company Goupil's sole representative in the UK. Anthony recalls that I was the most 'attentive', or rather 'insistent', salesperson he had met and also 'the only one who ever sold me a computer subsequently that I didn't need: new and with an Intel 80286 processor'.

Anthony doesn't always – in fact, quite often doesn't – totally endorse my outlook on life and/or work. It's important to have someone like that in your life, somebody who is prepared to challenge your most firmly held beliefs, and who will gaily slaughter a dozen or so of your most sacred cows.

As Anthony says,

*Mike and I have sometimes quite different outlooks on life. But actually we always get along splendidly, mainly, I think, because he saw early on that I definitely was not following fashion as far as creative ideas were concerned. He was open for suggestions and then took the more adventurous options, which made the presentation of information just that little bit more special. He has long had a maxim of always hiring someone better than himself, getting other people to do things that they know how to do better. Being able to identify that is a good aim.*

One area where Anthony and I have different approaches is in terms of wealth and prosperity. As he puts it,

*Around the time I met Mike I was becoming aware that what meant a lot to me personally was not worth a lot in financial terms in the commercial world. I had no formal business qualifications and had already spent ten years in the very different culture of serious classical music. I only wanted to earn money so I could finance creative work. I had been in an environment of state-funded orchestras; coming back to the UK was like being thrown into a completely different animal kingdom of scantily disguised vultures whose sole purpose seemed to be to feed off what others had created.*

*I've been evaluating the balance between material and spiritual wealth for years. Mostly at the invitation of the banks. One thing that is evident from living a 'creative' rather than a 'managerial' existence is the prejudging that one is subjected to at any place where funding may be available. Being an individual and remaining a nonconformist as far*

*as standard business practice is concerned is fine, spiritually.
As a result one becomes what looks like a semi-desperate
opportunist tied to the fickle creative needs of commerce,
and that doesn't fit well into business plans. My company
slogan happens to be 'Art despite technology', which tends to
represent what happens. It is probably more positive than 'art
despite too many commercial restraints'.*

This is how Anthony sums things up:

*Sure, I like consulting contracts from companies who
actually appreciate less conventional ideas. They provide
the elusive financial security that avoids me as a business
misfit. However, one doesn't always have the ability to
influence such things. Having family is great, though, and
being allowed to be creative through the financial support
of friendly clients (thanks, Mike) as well as other friendly
supporters is generally awesome. Just having ideas is
cheap and easy, but having the opportunity to create some
unique things that would not have existed without my own
intervention is most satisfying. Realising projects and gaining
the resulting spiritual wealth is primarily a matter of finding
partners who have a suitably admirable moral standing.*

Another example of difference of outlook is from Steve
Cliffe, a tech business entrepreneur who set up Ultrahaptics, the
company creating mid-air ultrasound controls. He describes
how the differences between us benefited the company:

*When my business partner Tom and I had the money in
place for Ultrahaptics, we needed a chairman on board.
The investment group had what was effectively an executive
search department and they sent over a stack of ten or so
CVs. We read through them and whittled them down to*

*three. Mike was in the 'No' pile – he didn't have experience in our specific area, even though he was within the tech industry. But the executive researcher pushed him, said we really ought to see him. So we added his name to the 'Yes' pile. We interviewed Mike last. After half an hour, Tom and I walked out, and we both said, 'It's him.'*

*There were two things that struck me: Mike thinks differently from Tom and myself. That has been borne out. I can go to Mike with a problem, give him four scenarios. And he will always come up with a fifth. The other candidates were very much more like us, with a similar history. They weren't clones, but they were close to us. We wanted somebody who was distinctly different, offering a positive challenge by giving us a different perspective.*

*Secondly, Mike is immediately likeable. A tough negotiator – I'm always glad he is on our side – but, however tough the debate, you remain friends. That ability to communicate is not always part of the tech business.*

*When you have a start-up there are many competing interests. The founders and the staff want to maintain equity, the investors want to maximise equity. Mike walks the tightrope beautifully, always gets to a solution, sees both sides of a problem, finds a middle ground, an integration: something which is far more difficult to achieve than people expect.*

## REMEMBER THE ORIGINAL
## MEANING OF 'PRIORITY'...

... it means 'the first thing'. And the only thing that's important. From the beginning of the twentieth century the tendency to make the singular 'priority' into the plural 'priorities' began to grow. Can multiple priorities co-exist? Probably not. So settle on the single priority that you want to hand on, bequeath and make your legacy. It makes everyone's lives more streamlined. There may be many things that are important, but keep focused on the most important thing.

When I left TelecityGroup I was faced with a challenge that I am sure faces many 45- to 60-year-olds who leave their roles: 'What the hell do I do now?'

Most of us will get there sooner or later. We will have the skill sets and the experience that help, but the truth is that the world is moving faster than we are and the belief that we can simply shift from one role to another as we might have done a decade ago is simply misplaced.

Companies want energy. Companies want youth. They believe (as I have alluded to before) that they can mould the right attitude with no experience into the right executor. I know. That's the way I saw life too.

So what's to become of the has-beens?

By the way, those of you between 35 and 45 who think this doesn't apply to you: the window of definition is coming down so fast that it will apply to you in a few years from now. So listen up.

The rate of change is exponential. In fact, I call it the rate of change *of change*. And that rate is accelerating ever more steeply. Technology is driving this. We cannot evolve as quickly as technology can, and those who fight against it will not only be unsuccessful in business, but ultimately unsuccessful in life.

I first realised this getting on for twenty years ago, when my daughter Eloise was born in Copenhagen just a few weeks before the turn of the century. It makes her very likely to be fortunate enough to witness first-hand three separate centuries on the planet.

When she was very young, before she could talk, I bought her a Fisher-Price toy telephone. It was an old-style phone with a rotary numeric dial and a handset on a cord, and of course wheels and eyes that rolled. She used to pull it along by a string everywhere around the apartment. It was one of her favourite toys.

One day I sat with her on the floor with my mobile phone and pretended to ring her phone. 'Brring, brring,' I said, with my mobile phone at my ear. 'Answer the phone, I am calling you.' I gestured to her phone. She kept looking at it, looking back at me, and looking at it again. She knew I was referring to it in some way but just couldn't understand why. And then it dawned on me. Although this was her favourite toy, for her it didn't represent a phone. She had never seen a phone with a rotary dial, or a cable to the handset. For her it was just a nice toy. All the phones she had ever seen looked like a standard mobile phone.

It shocked me to think that an object as iconic as a dial telephone, which I am sure anyone of my generation would recognise in an instant, was now, in just one generational step, completely forgotten.

Do not rely on your life experiences as a proxy for future generations. If you can, try to engage with the next generation – your kids. Understand what they like, why they follow certain things on social media, what is important to them and why it is different from your point of view. And perhaps aim to recruit your staff and grow your business in the same way.

## QR: AUGMENTED DISCOVERY

Click on the QR code opposite. You'll instantly download clips of me telling you more about each of these key points:

■ Long-term thinking is the key. Short-term thinking is driven by fluctuations, of business success or failure, but equally of emotions.

■ Hire staff based on whether you believe they will be able to adapt to change, to be flexible in their thinking, and be prepared to engage in a continuous learning process.

■ An automatic reflex is to promote staff within the discipline and expertise of their track record. In fact, placing them into new areas that demand fresh skills will help staff grow exponentially.

■ Try to avoid creating a work environment that is formed by clones of yourself. If you are going to demand an openness to continuous learning from others, then challenge your own comfort zone.

*'Our Earth is degenerate in these later days; there are signs that the world is speedily coming to an end; bribery and corruption are common; children no longer obey their parents; every man wants to write a book and the end of the world is evidently approaching.'*

Assyrian clay tablet – c. 2800 BC

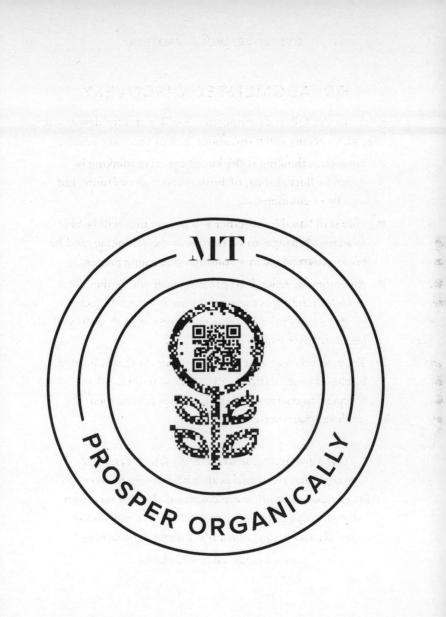

# Chapter 12

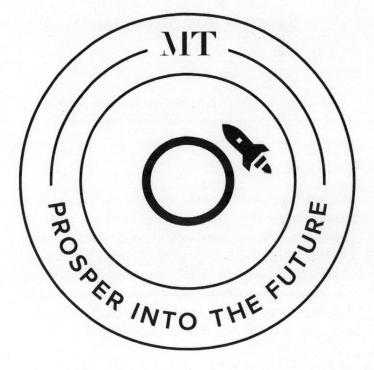

# PROSPER INTO THE FUTURE

## Success and succession

*'As much as we need a prosperous economy, we also
need a prosperity of kindness and decency.'*

Caroline Kennedy

The word 'prosperity' comes from the Latin 'prosperus',
meaning 'favourable' in the sense of good fortune. In time, it
evolved to have the additional sense of being affluent, of having
a fortune, being prosperous in terms of acquiring money.

Perhaps we should go back to its origins, and that suggestion of flourishing, of flowering, of realising potential, rather
than purely monetary gain. In this way we may be able to pass
on a sense of 'prosperity' that will genuinely enrich the next
generations.

## TREATING SUCCESS AND
## FAILURE THE SAME

*'Success is not final, failure is not fatal. It is
the courage to continue that counts.'*

Winston Churchill

*The Family Fang*, starring Nicole Kidman and Jason Bateman,
is a movie about a dysfunctional family. There is a resonance
in the film with Tolstoy's classic (and now so overused as to
be almost clichéd) opening line from the novel *Anna Karenin*,
'All happy families are alike; each unhappy family is unhappy
in its own way.' Nicole Kidman described the film as being
'about relationships, that delicate human interplay which can
so easily go astray. It's not just about parents and children and
art. It's about all of us – a cautionary tale about the damage
we can inflict on the people we love.' But somehow, out of a
string of mishaps and misunderstandings, something positive
emerges. The resolution comes out of left field, winging in on
that 45° angle.

When – like, it seems, 90 per cent of everyone I know –
I once accidentally smashed my phone, I wasn't sure how I
would survive, but in fact I lived without a phone for two
weeks, and it was OK. Although its absence made me really
appreciate the value of my phone when I did get a new one.

And then I lost my laptop during the writing of this book.
I felt stupid and embarrassed, of course, not least because I
hadn't backed up my material for several months. As a senior
figure in the data technology industry, that is a hard confession
to make. It wasn't that I had particularly sensitive information
on my laptop – although there were of course various commercial contracts and reports that might have been of some

value to competitors – but rather the fact that I generate a lot of material across the well over a dozen companies that I am actively involved with as a board director or chairman, and I download, collect and collate all kinds of items of interest.

I do have an excuse. It was all for love. I was flying into Heathrow on Valentine's Day. I had a quiet dinner arranged with Shalina, an oasis of togetherness during what had been a hectic, non-stop few weeks of travel and meetings. The flight had been delayed and I was desperate to get off the plane as soon as it landed. As we parked up at the arrival gate, and the seat belt light pinged off, I was up and out with my carry-on in a flash. In my desire to get home, I left my laptop snugly tucked into the magazine pouch. Despite contacting the airline and obviously knowing exactly the flight and seat number, it never turned up. I hope whoever has it now feels a tiny modicum of guilt.

Without the laptop I quickly had to lurch from despair to learning to live without it, and I made a huge mental note to carry on making back-ups. Then it occurred to me that this might also apply to my personal life: is there an equivalent of making a life back-up? Can we have milestones (like Polar expedition depots) that we can return to if everything goes pear-shaped? The family can be one of those safe havens.

I also realised that there was no need for techno-paranoia. Many people are frightened by the Cloud – we can hate it or embrace it. Those who are scared don't understand how it operates. They see it as a digital Big Brother. In fact, the risk that someone is monitoring you is minute. The more paranoid among us imagine that our information is of huge interest to other people. The reality is that the majority of our input is banal and mundane to the point of boredom, and the idea that someone would be spending 24 hours monitoring our every word is crazy. We would have to live in a fantasy police state where every person was being tracked by their personal spy every minute of every day – and then who would monitor the monitors? It's madness. It may be a shock to our egos, but Wikileaks really aren't that interested.

The top ten passwords in 2016, according to SplashData, which collates passwords from data breaches in America and Western Europe to build samples, were:

123456
password
12345678
qwerty
12345
123456789
football
1234
1234567
baseball

It really does make a mockery of 'online security'. Also, how many of us choose a password and use it for pretty well everything we do online that needs a password? It is like carrying a master key around that, once lost, opens every door in sight. There is so much we can do to improve our chances of not having our identities stolen, but in reality doing the basic stuff right will prove to be 99 per cent fine for most of us.

Life is like that. You can de-risk life significantly by just doing the simple things right. Eating well, sleeping well, the usual. We should carry on doing what we should do, and then try and deal with what surprises us as it happens.

Life is made up of a variety of ups and downs, in our family life, our relationships, our work, our emotions. I remember an advert which showed an ECG screen next to a bed monitoring a heartbeat and then becoming a straight line. Its core message was that if you are not experiencing ups and downs, then you are flatlining. Prosperity alone does not guarantee you will be happy.

There are extremely wealthy people who are deeply unhappy, and there are very happy people with very simple lives who have almost no material wealth. However, it seems to be the variation of ups and downs that creates the positive emotion – like the salesperson who gets rejected many times before they make a sale. If they made a sale every time, they would never experience the joy of success and of job satisfaction.

## CREATING TRUE LEGACY

Every year I go for a full MRI scan. Every element of my health is rigorously checked and tested. It is expensive, but the value for me is that I have no health insurance. I insure my car, of course, because I have to legally, but if I know I am healthy on an annual basis, then why should my insurance contribution subsidise the others? I do that through taxes and social security contributions. I see the MRI scan as a pre-emptive strike. I prefer to have an early warning system of any problems rather than paying the (potentially ultimate) bill, after the event. Let me reiterate Steve Jobs's final words: 'The most expensive bed we will ever stay in is our sickbed.' Let's avoid it if we can.

Legacy is increasingly an issue, as parents and grandparents have a greater life expectancy than ever before. The 'SKI' mentality – Spending the Kids' Inheritance – used to be a good punchline to a joke. Now it is becoming the norm. Other families hustle for legacy, scrimping and saving and 'doing without' to make sure that their children have resources to draw on.

What does this say about what we value: the value of our own lives vs our children's lives? One point of view would be to say that children have no value without their parents: they would not exist without them.

Or is it simply that we want the best possible start for them? The natural extrapolation is that generations progress financially, but are they actually happy?

There is a great song by Harry Chapin called 'Cat's in the Cradle'. It tells the lifecycle of a man who is too busy at work to engage as fully as he might with his son. In turn, his son grows up to repeat the cycle, with no time to spend with his ageing father. It's a very simple, yet powerful, illustration of how our own behaviours affect those of our children.

So much of who we are is influenced by our parents. We need to be very conscious of how and what we give our kids as life messages. I remember coming to a moment in my life where I realised that there were traits in my personality that I could identify with those of my father. Traits I didn't like. They included my attitude towards my son. I didn't like the fact that I recognised these negatives in myself and it was clear to see that the cycle would continue if I didn't do something to change things. I did, and it made my relationship with my son so much better.

## LEADING FROM THE CENTRE

Leadership is a Western concept. In China, for example, it is about centrality. Being at the centre rather than leading from the front is a concept worth considering.

In Chinese families, the younger members evolve from

being educated to driving the 'success' of the family, getting better jobs, making more money. Then they in turn become parents and later leaders of the family. As they move into retirement and become grandparents, it seems they take a more central role. In many cultures there is a 'soothsayer', who has an almost statesmanlike role, passing the baton of leadership to the next generation, but in a way commanding an authoritative position. Could this be a role for chairs of organisations?

In their own way, and in the context of the circumstances of the time, both of my own parents tried to protect me from harm and allowed me to feel loved. In my eyes they failed to a large extent. It took a long time for me to come to terms with that. My father passed away on the day of my mother's funeral, not having known that she had passed away a few days before. I did not go to either funeral. That is something I also had to come to terms with. It was a decision made out of frustration, anger, sadness. With a kinder view of life that tends to come of age, I perhaps would have made a different choice. Is that a typical example of the maturity a chairperson brings or should bring to a business, or the wisdom of the elders in a family?

While spoken words can burn deep and leave scars never to be erased, real agony stems from words unsaid. Courage, truth, loyalty, humility and compassion are vital but oddly uncommon human virtues.

In the instant moment of daily business, there is always also an element of looking forward on behalf of the next generation – and what to pass on, in terms of knowledge, structure and legacy of the business.

In modern times, family businesses tend to be better at this, with public companies finding it very challenging. Investors in listed companies are generally looking for short-term returns but will also punish companies for not preparing for the future. Why is this? It is because investors do not invest in a company because of what it is worth, but because of what it will be worth in the future. They can only sell their shares at a profit if a new potential investor is willing to buy them at a higher price, and that will only happen if they perceive even more value to come.

Is it possible for a business leader to achieve a perfect balance between the short and long term? By definition, you cannot, like a lens in a sophisticated camera, focus on two different distances at the same time. You need to change the game. You need to find the plan that integrates long- and short-term value.

Just like life.

## QR: AUGMENTED DISCOVERY

Click on the QR code at the end of this chapter. You'll instantly download clips of me telling you more about each of these key points:

- Rediscover and reconsider the true meaning of prosperity: not simply material affluence, but also a sense of flourishing fruitfulness and personal growth.

- Consider the Chinese concept of being at the centre rather than always having to lead from the front.

- Despite the demands of detail and the urgency of daily decisions, always try to bear in mind the requirements of the future, of creating a legacy for the following generations.

'Your work is going to fill a large part of your
life, so the only way to be truly satisfied is to do
what you believe is great work. And the only way
to do great work is to love what you do.'

Steve Jobs

# AFTERWORD

## Moving heaven and earth

A few weeks after it had been publicly announced that I would be leaving TelecityGroup, I was in a cab going to catch a flight to Canada to attend the wedding of one of my wife Shalina's cousins.

While we were on the way to the airport I took a call. I was being asked if I could change my plans and go down to Johannesburg in the next few days to discuss a potential deal. This was a significant opportunity, a deal that would turn out to provide an important cornerstone for my post-Telecity, independent, working life. Time was when I would probably have said yes without a second thought, rejigged all the arrangements and left Shalina to make my excuses as I disappeared. This time I refused. It was something of a first.

I told my contacts in South Africa that I had already made it quite clear that my week in Canada was going to be a family week, not a working week. As with all good Indian weddings, there was going to be an important, absolutely not-to-be-missed function on every single day of the week we were out there. There were precious few gaps in the programme.

Shalina was incredibly supportive, sitting next to me in the cab and flicking through the diary, trying to find out whether there was a gap that would allow me to make a lunatic, non-stop, round trip from Toronto to Jo'burg and back. It wasn't possible, so I turned down the meeting, rearranging it for another date, some weeks later.

Out in Toronto I took another call from a business contact. This time the invitation was to go to a dinner party in Washington DC on the Friday evening. He wanted me to meet a wealthy investor who was interested in funding a new venture. The contact thought my presence was important because I would be best able to articulate the shape and the vision of the venture by being there in person.

I told Shalina, and we looked at the diary again. It turned out that the Indian wedding ceremony function on the Friday was taking place in the morning, finishing at around three in the afternoon. The next event was a party on the Saturday evening starting at 7 pm. There was a small window, but a window nevertheless, since the flight from Toronto to Washington DC was less than two hours. Shalina told me I should go – she realised it was an important opening – as long as I got back in time for the evening event.

So I left the wedding event at 3 pm on the Friday, heading to Toronto Airport still dressed in my Asian wedding garb (although I did take off the turban). I jumped on the plane to Washington DC and turned up at a house near Reston, just outside the city. The dinner party included senior staff from the US Defense Department, people from Türk Telekom I had met before, a Finnish member of parliament and one of the bosses of DuPont Fabros, among many others. It was excellent, a valuable evening. I was glad I had been able to go – since it was a one-off – and was grateful to Shalina for helping make it happen.

After a night in a hotel, I met at 7 am with the other guys involved in the venture for a three-hour debrief. At 10 am I absolutely had to leave to get back to Toronto. The evening's function was probably the most important event of the wedding celebrations, and I had already promised my cousin months before that I would be there as master of ceremonies, introducing the bride and groom, all the family members, and keeping the festivities going.

I arrived at Washington Dulles International only to find that, due to an incident at Chicago air traffic control earlier in the week – a fire caused by some disgruntled employee that had caused hundreds of flights to be cancelled – there was still massive disruption because all the planes were in the wrong place.

The departure time for the flight to Toronto I had booked was being moved inexorably later and later: one hour, two hours, four hours. I started to panic. Then the screens announced a six-hour delay, which meant I would be turning up long after the start of the wedding party, if the plane ever took off.

I phoned a friend of mine, the only person I know in Washington who owns a private jet. I called him up and said, 'I'm really sorry. I know it's Saturday morning, and that you are spending time with your kids' – in fact, I could hear in the background that one of his children was asking for an ice lolly – 'but I need your jet.' He said, 'I'd love to help out, Mike. Nice to hear from you, by the way...' The only problem was, he told me, that his jet – a Bombardier – was in maintenance and, to rub salt into the wound, it was actually in maintenance in Toronto, Bombardier being a Canadian company.

He told me to wait, and he would call me back. Meantime

I was still trying to come up with an alternative plan, and had gone back out through airport security to see, unsuccessfully, if I could book onto another airline that I'd heard was flying into a local airport in Toronto.

My friend phoned me back. He had good news: 'A pal of mine, who rents part of my hangar, has got a small plane. He's on site, so if you want to jump into a cab and go to the Manassas airfield in Virginia, he will sort you out.' I rushed out through security again, grabbed a cab, reached the airfield, found the guy. His plane was tiny, like a crop-sprayer. But I was delighted to see any kind of plane as I thought I would, finally, be able to get to the wedding.

There was one last hurdle, though. He didn't have a co-pilot that day, which meant that for insurance reasons he was only able to take me as far as the Canadian border. The best he could do was get me to Niagara Falls. Fine. While he ran through the aeroplane checks, I arranged for a car to pick me up at Niagara Falls, take me through the border and then drive the 80-odd miles to Toronto. It was a scene straight out of *Planes, Trains and Automobiles*.

In the car I phoned Shalina, who was just about to get onto the coach bringing her and the family from their hotel to the venue. I asked her to bring my tux and everything else I needed. And, believe it or not, we arrived at the venue – me in the car from Niagara Falls, Shalina and all her family guests in their coach – simultaneously. I had ten minutes to get changed, freshen up and focus. I had made it. It was a kind of miracle.

And what did everyone say? 'Mike, you should have told us. We'd have understood that the flight was cancelled.' 'No, no,' I told them all. 'A promise is a promise. I will move heaven and earth to deliver on my promises.'

This story sums up the critical distinction between work/life balance and work/life integration. Balance would have been me saying to my contact in DC, 'I am here in Canada for a family wedding. I booked it months ago. So I am really sorry, but I can't come to the meeting in Washington.' That kind of balance means the scales have to tip one way or the other. Integration is different: creating the window to achieve both, whatever the obstacles.

Right from the beginning of the trip Shalina had been playing her part, even trying to see if I could get to South Africa and back, and then supporting me to go to Washington. My commitment was reciprocal. I would get back in time to play my part in her family's most important event of the year.

Getting back in time – however much things might conspire against me – was equally as important as going, not of secondary importance. It proved to me that Shalina and I had evolved a relationship that meant we would always try to accommodate each other's needs, priorities and shared ambitions.

For me this crazed journey – with a wonderful outcome – was a perfect example of how I believe work/life integration should function.

You live. You love. You work. You prosper.

# Acknowledgements

For **living**:
Billy, Gen and John for putting up with me on my journey to get to where I am.
My mother for putting me on this earth.

For **loving**:
Eloise, Nelson and Rose for their unconditional love.
Shalina for always being there for me when I need it; my love and my daily inspiration.
My mother-in-law Kiran for accepting me as part of the family from day one.
Friends including Niclas Sanfriddson, Rupert Robson, Stephane Duproz, Martin Essig, John Athwal, Sheetal and Ricky Kapoor and many more too numerous to mention.

For **working**:
Clare Grist Taylor, Peter Jones, Paul Forty, Rachel Nobilo and the team at Profile Books for seeing the potential in this book.
Philip Dodd, whose persistence and calm has yet again guided me through the process perfectly.
Donna O'Toole, Lisa Seymour and Anthony Morris for their great creative contributions.

For **prosperity**:
Fernando Chueca, Michail Zekkos and many others for helping to make the combination of fun and hard work also financially rewarding.
Rudyard Kipling for teaching me to view triumph and disaster as the imposters they both are.
Winston Churchill: 'Success consists of going from failure to failure, without the loss of enthusiasm.'

# About the author

**Michael Tobin OBE** is an entrepreneur, technology pioneer and philanthropist who is an acknowledged authority on leadership, management techniques and business innovation. The *Evening Standard* has called his story 'a life-affirming rags-to-riches tale'. As CEO of data centre provider TelecityGroup plc from 2002 to 2014, Michael successfully steered the company into the FTSE250, increasing its market capitalisation value from £6 million to £1.6 billion. He was nominated as Business Leader of the Year in the 2013 National Business Awards and in 2014 received an OBE for services to the digital economy. In 2014 Michael stepped down from TelecityGroup to pursue an independent role with multiple technology investments and non-executive director and chairmanship positions across four continents. He is a board member, chairman and patron of many charities, including Friends of The Loomba Foundation, The British Asian Trust, Cooperation Ireland, the Duke of Edinburgh Awards and the Make-a-Wish Foundation, and he is the founder of the annual CEO Sleepout event for Action for Children. In 2016 he completed 40 marathons in 40 days to raise funds for The Prince's Trust during the trust's 40th anniversary year. He is the author of *Forget Strategy. Get Results*. Michael lives in Bermondsey, London, a stone's throw from his birthplace.